I'M THAT GIRL

I'M THAT GIRL

JORDAN CHILES

With Felice Laverne

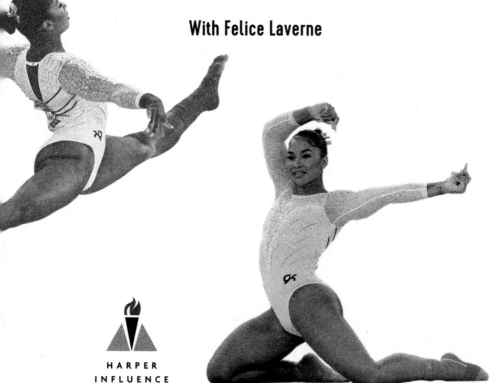

HARPER
INFLUENCE

LIVING THE POWER OF MY DREAMS

For Grandpa Gene and Auntie Crystal. I will continue to carry you with me into everything I do. I miss you both.

"If everything was perfect, you would never learn and you would never grow."

—BEYONCÉ

CONTENTS

FOREWORD

iles and Chiles—that's how the world knows us. Two of the Team USA gymnasts who wowed the crowds and brought home gold from the Paris Olympics in 2024. But my teammate Jordan Chiles and I have a friendship that goes further back than most fans realize—and is deeper than any catchy nickname could capture.

I first met Jordan years ago at a gymnastics training camp. Even then, her energy absolutely lit up the room. We lived in different regions of the country and were competing at different levels—we were four years apart in age, so I was at the elite senior level while Jordan was at the elite junior level. From the moment I first saw her gymnastics, I knew she was going to be great. She was athletic and strong with amazing form, and I just knew she was going to be a force to be reckoned with.

As our paths continued to cross on the competition circuit, it didn't take long for me to see she was as fun as she was talented. She was goofy, a little bit silly, loud, and outspoken—she reminded me of myself at her age. The other older girls and I were immediately drawn to her and were simply like, "Okay, we really like her!" We'd pull her into our rooms at training camps so we could all talk. She made us laugh—she always had Aly Raisman and me dying. And she loved being the center of attention. If we were listening to a song in our rooms, Jordan would be the one to say, "I'm gonna do this dance. Watch me!" That bubbly personality you see when she hypes up the crowd at competitions is definitely on display in private as well.

I think the two of us connected partly because we had so many similarities. We both started gymnastics late, around age six. I know six doesn't *sound* late, but a lot of Olympians or World Champions were tumbling in Mommy and Me classes as soon as they could walk. Some of our strengths and weaknesses in the gym were similar, and you kind of bond off that. We each had such power on tumbling and on vault, and we were both a little iffy on beam. Beam was our wild card back then. But her bars were always better than mine. Her form was so clean and beautiful and she could do pretty much every release—including the harder and less common ones like Shushunovas, Shangs, and Tweddles—which is kind of unheard of, particularly in girls of our small stature. I've always admired her for that.

I call her Jo and she calls me Mo—she's the first person to ever give me that nickname. So if I hear "Mo!" from across the gym, I don't have to wonder who's calling me. Our friendship grew over the years as we rose through the gymnastics ranks, and I think it's helped both of us become our best selves. When you have someone next to you who believes in the same dreams and goals, you can accomplish everything. Even if you have different styles.

Jordan's the team hype woman, willing to do anything out there to show her personality, while I get a little bit more in the zone when I'm competing. That's what works for both of us.

If we're chilling out together after practices, I'll cook dinner at my house and we'll watch movies. She loves Marvel and Disney, while I'm more of a love story and action girl. We get our lashes done, fix our hair together . . . Jordan can put in a weave, take out a weave, and do nails. She's a jack-of-all-trades! She can dance and sing and she loves trying to get me to do TikToks with her, which is *not* my favorite thing. We laugh about that.

Elite gymnastics is a high-stress sport, so those moments of downtime with people who understand what you're going through are so important. It's also crucial to watch out for each other's mental health, and Jordan and I make a point of checking in on each other to make sure we're feeling good. We always have talks about how we're doing, making sure we're both still going to our therapy sessions. I'll never forget the way she stepped up to fill in for me at one of the lowest moments in my life: when I had to withdraw from the Tokyo Olympics in 2020 because of a bad case of "the twisties"—losing your sense of where you are as you flip through the air. Suddenly—terrifyingly!—all eyes were on Jordan, but she rose to the occasion and helped the team bring home silver.

At the Paris Olympics last year, she went through her own devastating challenge. It was shocking and heartbreaking to see her stripped of the bronze medal she'd won for her floor routine. We know the performance she gave, and that she truly earned it. I am still shocked by how it all happened, as I am not aware of anything like that happening before in gymnastics. I know athletes have been stripped of medals before, but usually it takes a couple of years to happen and it's related to a doping issue or something like that. As far as I know, it's never been a week later that they just strip you of it. The rest of the team and I tried to support her, love her, and uplift her—the way they all did for me in Tokyo. Whether or not she gets back the medal, she'll always be a bronze winner in our eyes.

Through it all, Jordan has handled that whole situation with incredible strength and grace. Which doesn't surprise me, because that's who she is. On our Gold Over America Tour last fall, she put all the drama and disappointment behind her and just gave her best for the audiences. Who doesn't want to tour the country after you helped bring home a gold medal for the team? It was a celebration, and we all had so much fun.

I'm excited for readers of this book to get to know Jordan—the caring, funny, gifted friend who will be in my life long after our gymnastics careers are over. "I'm that girl" is the unabashedly bold motto she chose to live by in 2024. She absolutely is.

—Simone Biles

I'M THAT GIRL

1

A NIGHT TO REMEMBER

needed to score above *13.700* to get bronze.

When the Beyoncé medley I'd chosen for my routine concluded, I smiled and walked toward the Team USA seating area at the Bercy Arena. I had just completed my floor final, my last event of the 2024 Olympics in Paris—the event I was hoping would win me my first individual Olympic medal. *That was it. That's all I can do*, I thought. The adrenaline was still thrumming through my body. My white crystal-encrusted leotard was a little sweaty, but my hair was still neatly slicked back into a bun and tied up with a ribbon—more composed than I felt inside.

As the crowd roared and cheered, I sat down next to my best friend Simone—she's "Mo" to me, but the world knows her as the GOAT. We call this area "the kiss and cry"—that row of chairs you see us sitting on, on TV, when the cameras are getting close-ups of our faces as we await the judges' decisions. The cameras are watching your every move, waiting to capture any twitch of your face or grimace of disappointment. And then your score flashes up as the next competitor comes over to wait for *their* score. You end up either getting congratulated or blinking back tears as you congratulate someone else . . . the *kiss* and *cry*.

That night, August 5, I was the last gymnast to perform, so everyone was just waiting for my score. Years of training and preparation had come down to this. My heart thumped with anticipation, but I refused to get myself riled up about it. I had done what I could, and that's all I could do. I was exhausted—we all were. Floor is the most tiring of the four gymnastics events, and this was the last event on the last day. Instead of dancing around like I usually do, I was just trying to catch my breath.

As the cameras flashed, Simone turned to me, our heads down so the camera wouldn't catch our words, and asked, "How do you think you did?"

I leaned down to rub my numb ankles, which I'd landed hard on—"stung," as we say in gymnastics—in my last tumbling pass. "I don't think I did as good as I did in the team finals, but I feel like I did as good as Qualifications," I told her. My team finals score was *13.966*; in Qualifications it was *13.866*. "So I feel like I'm good."

She nodded solemnly. "Okay."

When they said my name to announce my score, my head and Simone's popped up at the exact same time to look at the leaderboard, where our scores and rankings are displayed. The suspense is intense: you see that graphic box under your name filling with green, stopping either lower or higher than the first-place finisher's graphic next to it. This time mine stopped lower, then turned red.

13.666.

It wasn't enough. Fifth place. No medal.

I looked away quickly and smiled pleasantly, remembering that I was on camera. I was disappointed but content. *Okay, that's all I can do,* I thought to myself, and I was fine with that, proud of myself and how far I'd come. At the time, the ominousness of that *666* didn't fully occur to me; later, it did.

What I didn't know was that less than a minute after my score was posted, my coaches, Laurent Landi and Cécile Canqueteau-Landi, had put in an inquiry disputing it. They knew that the difficulty value of my routine should have been 5.9, but they saw that 5.8 had been posted instead. Most people don't realize it, but it's pretty common for coaches to make inquiries after scores are posted. Inquiries can dispute the difficulty level awarded to your moves or any neutral deductions the judges may have taken off—for errors like stepping out of bounds. They can't dispute execution scores, meaning how well the judges feel you performed your routine. That evening, several inquiries had been put in by coaches of various countries, including ours.

Inquiries can be accepted or denied; if they're accepted your score can go up *or* down, or it can stay the same. In my career, my score has mostly stayed the same. So when Cécile came over to me and said, "I put in an inquiry for you," I didn't get my hopes up. I tried to stay busy—walking around, talking to Simone—as the seconds ticked by on the clock.

I was the first one of us to see my new score go up on the leaderboard—and I screamed. Jumped up and down and *screamed*. Simone was walking toward me, and Cécile was standing behind me, turned away from the board. They both looked at me, then at the leaderboard. I literally leapt into Cécile's arms, shrieking. I couldn't contain myself. I couldn't believe it! The inquiry had worked! After so many inquiry denials all day with other gymnasts, mine had been approved.

I fell to my knees, then rolled into a ball, sobbing with happiness. Cécile lifted me to my feet and pulled me into a hug. She twirled me around, cradled me in her arms like I was her own child. "We did it!" Simone jumped up and down behind us, grabbing me from Cécile to wrap me in a hug too. Around the arena, faces looked up to see that I was now in third place. I was the bronze medalist. In the crowd of tens of thousands in the stands, my dad beat his chest—*Let's go! Let's gooooo!*—and my mom fell to her knees, hands covering her mouth in thrilled disbelief. Everyone in Bercy Arena was on their feet. This was a history-making moment.

At the same time, Ana Bărbosu of Romania, who had been in third place, could be seen looking up at the scoreboard and seeing her ranking fall. I was rejoicing, completely unaware that she'd dropped the Romanian flag she was holding and was clutching her face, shattered and in tears. I knew she would be feeling the same anguish I'd felt just moments before, but I didn't realize she had started celebrating even though an announcement had been made to the arena that an inquiry was pending. For obvious reasons, competitors usually don't celebrate victory until the final score is posted. I'm not sure why Ana's coaches ignored that norm.

Something similar had happened at the 2012 Olympics in London. Romania was dominant in women's Olympic gymnastics in the 1990s and early 2000s, but by the mid- to late 2000s, Team USA was surging. At the London Olympics, Team USA's Aly Raisman won the bronze after an inquiry led to a change to her score, dropping a Romanian gymnast from the podium. The Romanian federation and fans were still sour about that one, and now—as they saw it—here it was happening again, just three Olympic cycles later. Little did I know the backlash that would create. I was heading into the center of a perfect, terrible storm.

But in that moment, as the press crowded excitedly around me, the Romanians' feelings in 2012 were nowhere in my mind. One NBC reporter asked, "The raw emotion when you realized you made the podium—we could all feel it. What's behind that bronze?"

"Honestly," I squeaked, my voice already raw from crying and screaming, "this is just a dream come true. This is my first time ever in an event final. Like we said, it was a 'redemption tour,' and I just wanted to come out and do the best that I could, so this medal means everything . . . I have no words but I'm very proud of myself."

There was no way that I could adequately express what I was feeling right then, the joy and relief and the memory of all the pain I'd endured to get there . . . *What's behind that bronze?* If only they knew.

2

A NAME TO LIVE UP TO

was named after Michael Jordan.

Before I was born, and put into gymnastics, and set on the amazing path my parents and I could never have envisioned, my mom, Gina, was already a sports head. She grew up running track and playing volleyball, basketball, and lacrosse, so gymnastics, swimming, basketball, football, track and field—you name it, she loved it. She looked up to the greats, as I do now, and she's always thought that Michael Jordan was the greatest of all time. The GOAT, no question about it. In any sport debate, she was always ready with Michael Jordan's stats. My dad, Timothy (who everyone calls Manny), always teased her about it. So when my first sister, the eldest of my four siblings, was born in 1993, my dad insisted, "Absolutely *no* Michael, no Jordan"—already knowing that my mom would go there.

My sister was named Jazmin instead.

As the years went on, and more pregnancies came, my father maintained the same stance. "No, Gina," he'd tell my mom. "No naming the next one Michael or Jordan."

My next sister, Jade, was born in 1995. My parents had no intention of having a six-year gap between us, but pregnancy was difficult for my mom. She hadn't been able to carry my sisters to term. Both of them tried to come into the world early—at around five months—then both held out until seven months after my mom was placed on bed rest for two months. The recovery from pregnancy was a long process for my mom's body. After Jade, she got pregnant but miscarried. She then got pregnant with twins but, devastatingly, lost them at five months pregnant. In all, they would suffer five or six losses. "I've never been good at carrying babies," she's told me, with a sad little laugh. "I just kept losing pregnancies."

After the loss of the twins, they were pretty much done trying. The losses were too devastating, and now Mom had fear mounting at each new pregnancy. *Will this one live? Will I have to face another shattering loss?* Emotionally, she really didn't think she could handle it—telling your family and friends that you're expecting and getting excited, fixing up a new bedroom and buying a slew of baby paraphernalia— only to then have your expectations dashed with another life lost. I have two older brothers in addition to my sisters: Tajmen (Taj) and Tyrus (Ty), who have a different mom but are very much a part of our family. Taj, like Jazmin, was born before my mom and dad were married; Ty was born during a period when my parents were separated. So my parents told themselves that two girls and two boys was just fine. They could be happy with that.

But then, six years after Jade was born, they learned they were expecting again. By now, Jade was starting school, and Jazmin was already in third grade. What my mom remembers feeling most strongly was *Here we go again. No, I can't get my hopes up.* They told no one that I was on the way. They wanted to avoid having to face the empathetic words and sad pats on the back they'd received after each loss. They didn't even buy anything for me during the pregnancy. Like two people standing in a wasps' nest, trying not to get stung again, they just remained calm and still, not wanting to do anything until they knew that this was actually going to happen.

But it turned out that I was the most normal pregnancy of them all—my mom carried me to term with no issues. She always says she didn't even know what a normal pregnancy was until she had me. They had gone through so much, both body and soul, that this outcome was more than they'd ever expected. To top it all off, I was born on Easter Sunday.

In photos from that day—April 15, 2001—they look absolutely "ridiculous," to use my mom's word—so stiff and formal. My dad is in an Easter Sunday suit, and she has a full face of makeup with her hair completely done—they'd been planning to head to church. My sisters had their hair braided neatly for Sunday service. I wasn't due until the next day, and they thought they could squeeze in one more service before I came—one more prayer for my safe delivery and one more time to praise God for how far they'd come in the pregnancy. My dad was actually on stage singing in church when my mom went into full labor. Everyone started frantically waving at him and he was so panicked he forgot where to go to get off the stage! He finally figured it out (go Dad) and drove my mom to the hospital. I was ready to greet the world, but I wasn't going to make things easy. My mom's blood pressure dropped, she passed out, and I was showing signs of distress, so they had to stabilize her and deliver me as quickly as possible.

As my father looked down at me—their miracle baby—in my mother's arms in that hospital bed, he stroked her hair and told her, "Boo, that was hard. But you did it. We did it. You can name that girl whatever you want."

"Jordan," she said resolutely. "I know she will do great things."

3

THE SURPRISE

At the time that I was born, my family lived in a two-bedroom apartment in Portland, Oregon. Sometimes my brothers, Taj and Ty, lived with us, sometimes not, but we were all raised together, went to school and family functions together, and we are all close. My parents instilled in us that we should always move as a unit—even as we had our sibling fights. "Family is everything," they'd say. "If you rise, everybody rises, and if we rise, you rise." They still say that, along with my dad's favorite: "Last name Chiles!" It's his go-to for getting us moving, encouraging us to meet challenges or just reminding us who we are. We've always *felt* like a unit, and we'd laugh when our friends tried to figure out how everyone fit into the picture. It was fun to leave them confused.

During my earliest years, my mom worked as a regional property manager, and our apartment was at one of the sites she oversaw. My father was a maintenance technician on the property. My parents lived paycheck to paycheck, and we lived in various apartments over the years as they worked to put themselves in a financial position to purchase their own home.

I was four when we moved into our house, a brand-new build on a cul-de-sac in Vancouver. It was a three-bedroom setup like the Huxtables' on *The Cosby Show*, with stairs leading up to the second floor from the back wall in the living room, and another set of stairs going down into the kitchen. My dad had always wanted a house like the Huxtables', from watching that sitcom growing up—and now we had one. The walk-in entryway was twenty feet high, and there was a basketball hoop in front of the house in the cul-de-sac. We stayed in that house all the way up until I graduated from high school.

Jazmin had her own room, but Jade and I shared a room when we first moved in—which, of course, she hated. No ten-year-old ever wants to room with their four-year-old sister, so you can imagine it wasn't all peace and love. I remember I wanted black and pink polka dots as the theme of the bedroom. Jade complained to our parents that this was the worst thing that had ever happened in her life.

My parents' bedroom was gigantic, taking up basically the entire upper level of the house. My mom was very interested in interior design, and it became her hobby over the years, so the house was constantly evolving—first carpet, then hardwood floors, painting projects galore, gutting the kitchen, adding on new rooms. A few years after we moved in, they used some of the space from their bedroom to build a whole other room, creating another bedroom that would later become mine, making the house a four-bedroom home.

I was a little sister with way too much energy, always on the go, always trying to figure out how to make furniture my personal jungle gym. There was something so freeing about jumping up and down on the sofa until I was breathless, after hours of being pent-up at my desk in school. I still remember the feeling. It was thrillingly fun for me, even as my parents would be yelling, "Get down from there! Stop that! We don't want you to hurt yourself." I could tell that my energy level was significantly higher than my siblings', but I never really thought much of it. They were old—practically grown-ups! Probably too old to remember how much fun jumping around could be.

My mom later told me that she and my dad were afraid the school system would label me hyperactive and try to put me on medication because I just couldn't sit still or pay attention in class. They didn't want that. My pre-K teachers had told them that I was struggling to stay focused, that I was hyperactive, and that they would continue to monitor me if it started to interfere with my ability to learn, alluding to an ADHD label but never officially putting one on me. I just wanted to be free, to leap and jump and explore my surroundings. I would be at my siblings' basketball and football games, or track and field meets, and just be all over the place with that much open space. Sports were a rule in our house—"You're not just going to be sitting around playing video games or doing nothing; get out and do something," my mom would say—so, I would race older kids and beat them, four years old beating a seven-year-old. My mom had it in her mind to put me in track and field, one of her favorite sports, when I got a little older. "She just needs an outlet," she told my dad.

They'd tried putting me in T-ball, on a team called the Pink Princess Ponies, or something like that. I'd don my giant pink helmet and gloves and be walking around looking like a bobblehead, like Chicken Little, in my oversized headgear on top of my tiny body. That's how I got my nickname, "Chicken Little," which we shortened to "Chick." My family often still wears #TeamChick gear to my meets. But I wasn't interested in being in the outfield. I'd be flipping around, not paying attention to when the balls flew my way, bored out of my mind. I needed to be right in the center of the action.

Because I had so much energy, I also *loved* being outside. We would take family trips, going camping and white water rafting. I learned later that they had to save up to take us kids on those trips. Eventually, my dad worked for the state, in social services, monitoring the interactions between kids who were taken from their homes and their families and trying to get the families reunited at some point. Things were still financially tight, but I never noticed—my parents always found a way to make it work. I loved those family vacations, but I also reveled in just being outside in our backyard. I would just be at one with nature. I remember one time I saw a dead hummingbird and went and picked it up. Nobody else in my family would have dared touch it, but I did with no fear. I was always interested in animals. Later in my childhood, I wanted to become a zoologist.

The year I was six, my mom went on a work trip for an entire week, leaving my sisters and me at home with our dad. Much to Dad's dismay, the fact that he was on his own with us didn't stop me from being my usual self, leaping off the furniture and somersaulting on the couch. One day after school, I was in the kitchen cartwheeling as he made dinner. He was the cook of the family because my mom didn't really like cooking. She'd do it because she needed to feed her family, but she never found joy in it. My dad did. Lasagna, red or green chile, or sausage sauteed in barbeque sauce over rice were some of my favorites. And pizza and hamburgers, of course.

Even over the delicious aroma of his cooking, I could smell the Hawaiian Breeze plug-ins my mom was obsessed with. She always wanted the home to smell good and be in order. *Law & Order*, my parents' fave, was on the TV in the living room.

"How was your day at school?" my dad asked me as he cooked.

"Fine!" I responded, still flipping around him.

"Well, what did you learn?" he asked.

But I never stopped or slowed down to answer him. I just kept cartwheeling and flipping around, until he came over and pinned my hands to my sides to stop me from moving. "Jordan, calm down, Chick. Now, tell me, how was your day in school?"

The thing was, being able to jump around gave me an outlet to express myself in a way that I couldn't yet with words. So, while I wasn't shy, and I could talk a mile a minute about what my friends and I had done at school, I was never as expressive when asked direct questions. I had always been "dry," as my mother calls it, because I've just never been a very descriptive person, and I would exhaust my parents most days after school when they tried to pull information out of me.

"How are you doing?" they'd ask.

"Good," I'd respond simply.

"How was your day?"

"Fine."

"What did you eat?"

"Food?"

I was more comfortable talking if it was on my own terms or if I could move around, I don't know why. On my head, upside down . . . When my dad pinned my arms down to get me to stop moving, my words stopped too. I went silent, looking up at him. As soon as he let me go, I went back to happily flipping, now able to answer his questions about school. This continued all week.

One of my mom's favorite stories to tell is how, when she got back to town from that work trip, my dad went to the airport to pick her up while we were all at school. He helped my mom with her bags and, as soon as she had the door closed in the passenger seat, turned to her with a look on his face like *she had me running for my life all week.* He told her, "I've been thinking . . . we should sign Jordan up for gymnastics. I've already done some research."

They went directly from the Portland International Airport to Naydenov Gymnastics in Vancouver, Washington, eleven miles away. No kidding, they didn't even stop at home first. They signed me up for Tuesday and Thursday classes for forty-five minutes each. Later that day, when they came to pick me up from school, I ran to the car, my backpack bouncing against my back, my hair pulled up into an Afro puff atop my head—one of my favorite hairstyles at the time. I was happy to be out of the classroom and back in the March sunlight.

When I got in the car, I saw that both of my parents were there. Usually, just one of them picked me up, so that was strange, but I hadn't seen my mom in a week, and I was excited to see her. They both turned around in their seats in front of me. "We have a surprise for you!"

"A surprise?! Oh my gosh, yay, what is it, Mom?!" I was so giddy, trying to think what the surprise could be, especially when my mom pulled out one of my dad's shirts and tied it around my eyes, blindfolding me.

"You'll just have to wait and see!"

As we drove toward my surprise, I ran through all of the things I thought it could be. A birthday party? Probably not on a school day. A pony? Well, that would be too big to live in the house with us. *What could it be?* By the time I'd settled on an idea, now sure I knew what the surprise would be, the car was stopping. My parents led me into a building, sat me down on a bench and took off the blindfold.

"Ta-da! Surprise!" they shouted, excited. "We enrolled you in gymnastics classes!"

What I saw in front of me was not what I had been expecting. Not by a long shot. It was just a gym. My six-year-old eyes started welling up, and within seconds I was crying. This clearly was not the reaction my parents had expected, just like this was not the surprise *I'd* expected.

"But I thought . . ." I managed to get out through my tears, "I thought you bought me a puppy!"

*   *   *

Over the weekend, my parents kept talking up the gymnastics class, and I forgot about the puppy and got excited. In fact, I wouldn't stop talking about my surprise. Now I could meet other kids who liked to flip around just like I did—that didn't sound half-bad. It had to be better than T-ball.

On Tuesday afternoon my mom picked me up from school and took me to my first class. As we walked in, I saw colors everywhere: blue floor mats and red runways and yellow steps up to the still rings, like a Crayola playscape. There were no other Black girls in the room, but at that age, I didn't notice. It was the same at school, and not something that really registered with me. Only later would I realize that faces of color were rare in gymnastics in general. And that the lack of diversity would make my road harder.

My mom released me to the coaches, and I happily followed them into the gym while she went to sit in the mezzanine viewing area to watch with the other parents. As the coaches introduced themselves, they touched my arms and commented that I already had muscles.

"Wow, Jordan! Do you already play sports?"

"T-ball," I replied, with a shrug. "Also track. I like running."

In that forty-five minutes, I showed them what I could do. They put me on a trampoline and told me to just jump. I remember doing toe touches and all kinds of leaps, giggling, giddy. Then they put me on the uneven bars and let me play around there as they watched and spotted me. Some of the other kids, I noticed, couldn't even pull themselves up on the low bar. The coaches asked me to do cartwheels on the floor, and they didn't have to ask twice. The class flew by so fast, I felt I'd barely had time to get started. I was already hungry for more! At the end, one of the coaches walked me over to my mom.

"How long has your daughter been in gymnastics?" the coach asked.

A confused look crossed my mom's face. "Ummmm, forty-five minutes," she replied.

Now it was the coach's turn to look confused. "Wait, what? Are you serious?"

"This is literally her first class."

The coach's demeanor changed. She shifted her body weight, looking down at me as I looked up at her. "Wow, well, I mean, she's really coordinated for a child of this age. Very aware of her body and how to move it. I put her over there on the bars and she was already able to do a pullover. You know, pulling herself up and over the bar? She knew how to do it and wasn't scared at all. I really think that you should consider putting her into a pre-team—those feed into competitive teams."

My mom laughed. "Nope, absolutely not," she said. "We're just here to, you know, get all of this energy out of her. Give it someplace to go, an outlet." She smiled politely, taking my hand. "So, yeah, thank you, but we're good."

The coach frowned. I turned around and stared at her as my mom led me away. The coach was watching us go.

*   *   *

Two days later, I jumped excitedly into the car after school, already hyped for what I knew was coming next. Time for gymnastics class number two! My parents were happy that the first class had gotten out some of my energy. I was still a ball of *go* when I got home, but a little bit less so. They were satisfied with that.

That Thursday, I did much of the same in class, but there were different coaches there this time. And at the end of that class, the same thing happened. This new coach went to talk to my mom. "I think you should really have her try out for pre-team."

"Please, Mom, please!" I begged. *"Please, please!"* I jumped up and down and even made my puppy-dog face. I didn't know what pre-team was, but if it meant I got to do more of what I was already doing, I was in! The coach said I needed to know how to do a back walkover in order to qualify for pre-team, but that sounded easy enough, whatever a back walkover was. I was so excited about this new world that I'd been introduced to.

"We'll think about it," my mom told the coach, and again, took my hand and walked away.

In the car, I continued begging. *"Please, please, please,* Mom! It sounds *so* fun!"

"Jordan," she said, putting her seat belt on. "They say you can't even be on pre-team unless you do a back walkover. I don't know what that is, but I guess it takes a while to learn."

Takes a while to learn? I'd show them. I asked my uncle, who knew gymnastics, what a back walkover was and he showed me: you point one leg in front of you and arch your body backward, placing your hands on the ground while kicking your legs over your head to land back in a standing position. I practiced over and over at home and mastered it in a day.

After that, the coaches were even more serious about the pre-team conversation. They could see something in me that I couldn't yet see in myself. My parents gave in, I tried out for pre-team, and I made it. Not only did I make it, but I had two of the gym's higher-level coaches battling for whose team I would eventually be on. I didn't really understand what all of that meant, but it felt good that adults were fighting over me!

The way USA Gymnastics (USAG) training is set up is kind of complicated: there are ten levels with set programs for each level, and you need to master certain skills to progress from one to the next. Pre-team is essentially levels 1–3, although my gym just lumped the three levels together into one pre-team. There are meets at both pre-team and 4–6 levels, and at 4–6 you can qualify for state meets, but it isn't until level 7 that you can go to regional meets. The two Naydenov Gymnastics coaches who started taking on kids at level 7—Coach Paul and a woman we'll call Coach X, for the purposes of this book—were the ones already signaling they wanted to work with me. We had to choose between them in advance because the gym had two level 4–6 teams, one feeding directly into Paul's team and the other into Coach X's. "Coach X's team, with her coaching partner, Dimitri, is the very best in the region, if Jordan ever wants to do anything serious with gymnastics," the gym's coaches told my mom.

My parents still weren't completely sold on this serious gymnastics thing for me. How had "Jordan needs to let off some energy" turned into this? But I was so enthusiastic, and I liked Coach Trish, the one whose team fed into Coach X's. We decided to choose that path and see how things went.

4

IN IT TO WIN IT

come from a close-knit but very competitive family—the kind of family where a board game is *never* just a board game. A friendly footrace down the block was never just that—there were always bragging rights on the line. A good-natured game of basketball with my siblings and my dad, outside in our cul-de-sac, always came loaded with laughter and trash talk. And me being the youngest of five kids, well, I had to be ready to show up and show out if I ever wanted to beat one of those bigger kids. I had to fight for every position they gave me and every victory I earned. There's no way that they were going to go easy on me just because I was the baby.

I remember a time we were all playing Scrabble as a family, around the time I started gymnastics. My mom put down this big word, like *encouragement*, and scored a ton of points. One by one, my siblings and my dad all put on their thinking caps and went hard, putting down word after word that I didn't even understand—and certainly didn't know how to spell, like *penalty, arrangement, accommodate.* My sister Jade was a bookworm, and though my brothers hated homework, they played too. Word after word, they built off of each other's think-on-your-feet genius as the living room filled with laughter and high fives. When it came to my turn, I squinted my eyes, thinking and thinking.

"Mom," I asked. "How do you spell *category?*"

"Mmm-mmm!" she chided with a laugh. "You better get up and get that dictionary and figure it out, girl. No gimmes around here!"

I wound up rolling my eyes and just putting down the word *cat.* It was so annoying at the time, but my mother always told us we needed to learn that if you wanted something in life, you had to work for it and earn it. I was about to prove to everyone just how thoroughly I'd gotten the message.

*   *   *

Starting when I was in pre-team at Naydenov, our gym's booster club would organize meets with other local gyms. At these meets, we gymnasts would perform all four events— vault, beam, floor, and bars—but at a lower skill level than the more advanced gymnasts. For vault, for example, we would jump off the springboard and vault to the mat, rather than using the vault table, and land on our backs on the mat. It was all about learning and performing the basic skills so we could build on those skills to become better gymnasts. In pre-team, we all got participation ribbons at these meets, but by the time I got to level 4—just months after my very first class—we were scored individually and we'd have medal ceremonies.

At this time, I didn't really understand what the scores meant. "I got a seven hundred eighty-five!" I'd yell excitedly to my mom when we got in the car to go home. Really, that was a *7.85*, and that wasn't very good at all. At age seven, I was just out there having fun, meeting other girls, and loving jumping around on the tumble tracks. Coach Trish instilled in us that it was most important to learn your skills well and have fun. A lot of coaches don't push the idea of scores at that age because it can be emotionally unhealthy. Gymnastics was now one of the highlights of my week, but I still didn't know exactly what *competition* entailed.

At these meets, I would sit on the floor talking and laughing with the other girls after I did my routine, not really paying attention to what was going on. But then I started noticing that some of the other, mostly older girls would have their names called to go stand on the podium and get recognized, but my name was never called for that. I became hyperaware that there was something I was missing out on. Meet after meet, I'd sit on the floor during the awards ceremony, poised to leap up and run to the podium as soon as my name was called. But it never was.

Finally, I went over to my mom after a meet. "Why do the other girls keep getting to go up there," I asked her, "and they don't ever call my name?"

To this day, my mom says that this was one of the hardest conversations she ever had to have with me about gymnastics. How do you tell your child that they aren't very good, or aren't the best, at something they love?

"Well, here, come sit down, Jordan," she told me, and I took a seat next to her on the bleachers. "See, those girls are getting called up there because their scores were very good."

"Okay . . ."

"And . . ." She hesitated, rubbing my shoulder. "Well, baby, yours just aren't quite up there yet. But that's okay, we're just having fun, remember?"

I got caught on her first sentence and blew past the second one. "What do you mean 'my scores'?" In all of these months of gymnastics, I'd never once stopped to consider scores or rankings.

"Well, babygirl, you're all getting scored when you go out there. A ten is the highest score you can get, and those girls whose names are getting called all scored in the nines. You, well, you have been scoring in the sevens. But those are older girls, and they've had more time to practice and learn."

My little stomach absolutely plummeted, somersaulting in my chest. What I heard was that those girls out there were *beating* me. They were doing *better* than me. Everything had been *fun* up to this point, but once my mom explained this, I knew I needed to really lock in. I remember it just clicking in my head. As the youngest of five, I'd seen that, yes, sports could be fun, but you also wanted to *win*. I had to start winning.

I turned to look back over at the now-empty podium and vowed to myself that I would get my name called and be up there, even if I was competing against older, bigger girls. I was only seven, but gymnastics had become more serious for me.

*   *   *

It didn't take long for me to go from never hearing my name called to hearing my name called *a lot*, and I reached level 5 soon after reaching level 4. I would watch the older gymnasts at Naydenov, the girls I looked up to, and try to replicate what they had done. I focused especially on Destinee Davis, the only other Black girl at the gym. She was on Coach X's team and she was good—I was nowhere near her level, but I copied her. I was learning that to be the best you had to work like the best. I started making up my own floor routines at home.

At level 5, I was standing on that podium pretty regularly. I was getting better and better, but my parents were always careful to remind me that sportsmanship mattered as much as medals. "Nobody wants to be around a good gymnast who's an awful human," they would tell me. "Regardless of where you're at on that podium, be happy for everyone and congratulate the person you beat and the person who beat you." As I started beating girls who were taller and older than me, I'd give them a hug or a high five, and they would just roll their eyes at me. Who *was* this little seven-year-old beating all these older girls?

It was during that year, after I started in gymnastics, that I experienced my first overtly racist incident. We were at a meet in the suburbs of Seattle, about a two-and-a-half-hour drive from Vancouver. (My USAG region, Region 2, included Washington, Oregon, Alaska, Hawaii, Idaho, and Montana). At this point, everyone at my gym was getting excited about me because I was moving up the levels so fast. And now my whole family was involved in my passion:

my aunties and uncles, brothers, sisters, and grandparents would come to my meets, and so would our family friends. Everyone drove up to Seattle, and I loved seeing them in the stands cheering me on.

I was the only Black girl at this meet, but that wasn't unusual, and as I've said I never really thought about skin color at that age. I was with the other girls, preparing for the action to begin, when a white woman I'd never met came down from the bleachers and moved swiftly toward the area where I was about to perform. "Get that *thing* off the floor," she yelled. "She doesn't belong with our girls." I remember hearing her, but not really paying attention. I had no idea she was referring to me. But then I noticed that the whole gym had stopped to watch her. "Get that thing off the floor!" she kept screaming. "She doesn't belong with our girls!" She was only feet away from me and pointing in my direction. That's when I realized that she was talking about me.

The director of the meet tried to get the woman to stop screaming, but she would not be calmed or silenced, and the police had to be called to escort her out. Throughout the entire experience, I felt numb, unable to fully process what was happening. Why was this woman screaming at me? Why did she feel I didn't belong with the other girls? What about me had made her so disgusted?

I was mortified and humiliated that this woman had called me a *thing* in front of all these people. What was worse was that other parents seemed to agree with her. From the gymnasium floor, I couldn't hear the other parents' reactions, but my family could. "I mean, the girl *is* out of place," some agreed, while others wondered who my coach was and whether this was really the appropriate time and place to "make a statement."

Their words suggested that I couldn't possibly be as talented as their children—that I had no place there in that sport. My parents called on the meet director and host to intervene and protect me. None of the other parents stood up for me, though my four-foot-eleven mother didn't let much time pass before she was toe-to-toe with the woman, telling her forcefully to stop. I could feel the other girls' eyes on me, as I stood there completely frozen in shock. The police finally showed up and escorted her out of the building.

After the meet, we got a letter from the hosting gym and from the Region 2 president sent to our house, saying, "We apologize that this was your experience"—but no words promising to protect me at future meets. My parents decided not to explain to me the racial nature of the woman's attack; I was just too young, and they didn't want me carrying that emotional baggage around with me. They told me that the woman was being ugly, a term they often used to describe bad behavior, and tried to brush it off. But from that point on, they understood that my participation in gymnastics would come with hardships that the other girls wouldn't have to face, that just my being there was somehow political and could cause controversy. As my parents, they did everything they could to shield me from this reality, but there was only so much they could do.

Despite their best efforts, I was permanently scarred by that experience. From then on, I vaguely understood that I was different from the other girls, and treated as such. As long as I remained in gymnastics, people were going to look at me as an outsider at best and a threat to be kept down at worst.

*   *   *

By the time I was eight, I had skipped level 6 and reached level 7. I'd mastered all the new skills I needed to get there—like a "flyaway," which is a dismount flip off the bars. Level 7 is when gymnastics starts becoming really competitive; you are now eligible to compete in regional meets. At level 9, you can participate in state regionals and eastern and western Nationals, depending on where you live in the country. At level 10, you're eligible to compete at the National Championships. If you're good enough, Nationals is when the eyes of college scouts and National Team coaches are on you, potentially leading into more elite gymnastics or to college scholarships. With all of this at stake, many families opt to have their kids focus more on their sport than their schooling.

This became a point of contention between my parents and Coach X early on, before they even accepted me onto their level 7 team. Coach X had seen that I was winning the meets I'd been to, with my renewed focus on scoring—and scoring well. Sometimes Dimitri would pull me out of the lower levels to train with the level 7s, and in 2008, Coach X invited me to an Olympics viewing party with the older girls, which made me feel pretty special. Coach X saw such potential in me that she pushed for me to move to online or homeschooling so that I could devote more time to gymnastics training. This, I would learn, was fairly normal for families who wanted their kids to be elite gymnasts. But my parents were adamantly against it. Not only were they concerned about how well I'd do in an online school setting, since I needed to be really interested in what I was learning to fully get into it, they also wanted me to maintain a normal life as I grew up, elite gymnastics or not. I was a very social kid, and I needed to interact with my peers outside of the gym as well as inside. Again, my parents reminded me, "We'd rather raise a good human than a good gymnast, and if that means gymnastics goes away, then that's what that means."

In fact—though of course I didn't know this at the time either—this wasn't the first point of contention between my mom and Coach X. Coach X was very blunt and, often, simply rude, in a way that her partner, Dimitri, was not. Maybe it was a matter of differing communication styles in Romania, where she was from. I don't know. My mom later told me that the first thing out of Coach X's mouth the day they met, on the floor of Naydenov Gymnastics, was "Is she your kid?"

From her tone and body language, my mom believed Coach X was asking if I was biologically hers. My dad is Black, and my mom is Latina, so her skin color is lighter than mine, and Coach X was bluntly demanding to know if I was adopted. My mom, clearly annoyed, looked over at me working with one of the other coaches on the floor. I was proudly wearing the two Afro puffs that my mom had styled atop my head before practice. As a woman in an interracial relationship, my mom had experienced this kind of intrusive and offensive question before.

"I know she doesn't look like me," she responded, "but that's a terrible question to ask someone."

Coach X was unfazed. "Well," she replied matter-of-factly, "there's a lot of adopted kids in this sport. I'm just looking at how short you are"—she paused, giving my mom the once-over—"to see if this is something she'd even be able to do long-term before we accept her onto our team. I just want to see if she's going to stay small. Sometimes these girls start off good but then they get older and their bodies change and they can't do gymnastics anymore."

My mom laughed that one off. "Oh yeah, she's going to stay small. You should see her dad." My mom is four eleven, and my dad is five six. Height wasn't really in the cards for me, and to this day I'm five feet myself.

There's nothing inherently wrong with wondering about a young gymnast's future height. The average height of a female Olympic gymnast is four feet nine inches, as compared to five feet four inches in the general population. I was the runt of most groups I was in back then, including gymnastics. Shorter gymnasts, it turns out, can actually have trouble getting good scores for height and distance on vault, but we also often have less difficulty on the uneven bars. And we're less likely to run out of space for our tumbling passes on the floor or beam. So it wasn't the topic of height that offended my mom, it was the way Coach X so casually asked if I was her biological child. And the offensive questions just kept coming.

"How much money do you make? What do you do for a living?" Coach X asked. My mom didn't know what to say. "This is an expensive sport," Coach X continued. "If you work for a nonprofit or something, you won't be able to afford it."

My mom has always thought that the strange start to the

relationship could have been a bad omen of what was to come. But when she asked around, everyone who was part of the gymnastics community said that we should not let Coach X's brusque manner get to us. *That's just how she is. It's a cultural issue. But she's the best, and if she wants Jordan, you should definitely go for it! That's just how things are in this sport.*

* * *

When I joined Coach X and Dimitri's team at level 7, I had moved from being in "compulsory" gymnastics, where the elements are all predetermined (levels 4–6), to what's called "optional" gymnastics (levels 7–10). "Optional" means each gymnast performs a unique routine tailored to their strengths and abilities. There are still required skills and elements, but you have more freedom to choose how you perform them, the choreography and so on. Needless to say, it's also a lot more intense. I started being in the gym from noon to around seven thirty p.m. Monday through Friday, with just a ten-to-fifteen-minute snack break. I had to be up at around six in the morning for school, and I was homeschooled in one or two classes every year so that I could leave school early to go to the gym. (The homeschool classes changed depending on my class schedule but they were usually in science or social studies.) My parents would make me a snack pack—fruit, carrots, pretzels, and a half sandwich with a piece of chocolate as a treat—and then drop me off at gymnastics.

When I got home, dinner would be ready. Every one of us kids was in a sport—Taj and Ty were in basketball, track, and football; Jazz and Jade played volleyball and basketball and did track—so we didn't always get to have family dinner together. I'd say my prayer over my meal with my parents and then scarf it down—or sometimes I just ate in the car on the way home. Then homework, then time for bed. Saturdays were half days, and Sundays I had church. My parents had become pastors at According to His Word Worship Center in Vancouver, Washington. This Easter Sunday baby was raised as a PK—a pastor's kid—and our nondenominational church and prayer were a big part of my life.

I'd gone from forty-five-minute classes to get my energy out to gymnastics becoming a full-time job in about eighteen months. My mom had warned me that my new schedule would be tough. "Jordan, are you sure you want to do this? Just understand that this is going to interrupt a lot in your life. There are going to be things that you want to do that maybe you're not going to be able to do."

I remember telling her, "I want to do this. I want to become an Olympian one day, Mom." I had started watching the greats before me, like Dominique Dawes and Shawn Johnson, on YouTube, and I was beginning to envision myself performing for cheering crowds of tens of thousands. Dominique is Black and Shawn Johnson has a muscular build similar to mine—that allowed me to picture myself in their shoes, following in their footsteps. I would have to work hard, I knew, but maybe I could get there too. My mom was wary, but she let me follow my gymnastics-crazy eight-year-old heart. She trusted me with that decision.

I was honestly thrilled to be in the gym more often. *This* was what I wanted to do, all day every day. But the expense,

I didn't know or understand at the time, was becoming a huge strain on my parents. As Coach X had warned, gymnastics is an incredibly expensive sport, and the cost only balloons as you get better. To really compete, you need to spend thousands on coaching, professional gym access, and eventually travel. Booster clubs, led by parents, deal with the expenses for the competitive season—from leotards to travel for the coaches and the gymnasts, not to mention the per diems for the coaches and meet fees. The booster clubs add up the expenses for the year, and then the parents pay equal shares. This doesn't even include equipment fees and physical therapy if you need it. As for leotards, each one might cost $300, and you only wear it for one season. Coach X wanted us to all stand out at competitions, so our leotards would often be customized and adorned with Swarovski crystals. When I was first starting out, back in early 2008, it cost $400 a month just to train at my gym, not to mention all the other costs—a tall order for a family that was already working hard to make ends meet.

I don't know what they would have done if my uncle Joe hadn't offered to help out by paying half of my expenses. They alternated who would pay each month, my uncle or my parents. Coming from such a big and loving family, I was able to benefit from having a village who was invested in me and my success. The support was emotional even more than financial. My Auntie Crystal, my dad's sister, was always so excited about my gymnastics. She used to call me her "shero" because I was so determined to follow my dreams no matter how many obstacles were put in my way. And my mom's dad, my grandpa Gene, might have been my absolute biggest fan. He was so nervous for me once I really started doing competitions that he couldn't even watch them on TV, much less in person. He thought I'd be able to feel his nerves in the audience somehow and get more nervous myself! I thank God every day for both of them, and for the many other strong arms that have held and helped me along the way.

5

THE GOING GETS TOUGH

On Coach X's team, I was an exception in many ways. Most of my teammates were preteens or even in high school; I joined when I was eight. Unlike me, they were being homeschooled so they could prioritize their gymnastics. And while I was still fresh-faced and excited about this new sport, some of them had been at it for years, reaching higher and higher levels simply because that's all they'd ever done or known. Some of them hated gymnastics after so many years of being in it, but now they were in so deep that continuing on felt like the only way. For many of them a college scholarship was the goal, given the long odds of any of us reaching the Olympics.

In addition to being the baby, I was also one of only two Black girls on the team (nothing new there). Gymnastics has always been a mostly white sport. Founded in 1881, the Fédération International de Gymnastique (the International

Gymnastics Federation, in English) admitted only European countries: Belgium, France, and the Netherlands to start. As time went on, FIG grew to be the single most influential governing body of the sport of gymnastics, creating and enforcing the rules, systems for scoring, and aesthetic expectations. Because of the sport's European roots, most gymnasts were white, and their physical characteristics were held up as the ideal. Coach X clearly wasn't about to broaden her views of how a successful gymnast looked. I'd come into the gym with my hair styled in two Afro puffs, and she would look at them and sneer, "You look like you have two heads." To my mom she said, "This is not 'the elite international look.'" As I got older, I realized she probably meant it wasn't the *white* look.

My sister Jazmin would do my hair for my meets, a beautiful ritual for us. I would sit between her legs as she braided or pulled my hair into ponytails or Afro puffs. Sometimes she would tuck my puffs into balls, one on either side of my head. We called those "giraffe ears"—that was my "competition hair." I didn't really wear that style for everyday. As soon as my hair was brushed up into those giraffe ears, it was *game on*. Hair is both deeply personal and political for Black girls and women. It is a symbol of our heritage, but it also elicits reactions from those who aren't Black. Having people ask to touch our hair, exoticizing and othering us, teaches us a lot about the world we live in and how we should move within it. It can affect how we feel about ourselves if we aren't given the emotional tools to counter those responses. I'm proud of my hair, the way I'm proud of my family and proud to be a Black woman, and that has never changed. How I style my hair for gymnastics still matters so much to me because I want my hair to be an extension of my personality. Yet when I was starting out and Coach X would glare disapprovingly at whichever style I had chosen that day, all I knew was that it hurt.

But it wasn't going to stop me.

*   *   *

One of my first competitions at level 7 was a meet in Seattle early in the season, in December of 2009. It was a competition that, if I won, would offer me the opportunity to travel to Florida, to Disney World, with other winners from our region to compete against other regions. At this point, I was spurred on by the competitiveness I'd been raised with and by my desire to make it to the global stage. And, to hear my mom tell it, I was *ripped*. I'd always had muscle tone and definition from all the flipping around I did, but now my body was starting to change. My mom says I had a twelve-pack.

When I was older, she told me about a time when she was watching me practice, sitting in the mezzanine with the other parents. "They're most definitely giving that kid steroids," she heard one mother say to another, unaware that this Latina woman sitting nearby was my mom.

"Oh, feeding them to her like Skittles, probably." The other woman snickered back. Of course, that wasn't the case.

I was super excited about the possibility of the Disney World meet. I mean *super* excited! Before the competition, I put on my aqua-blue "leo" (we almost never say "leotard"). It had big white waves across it, with one arm that was

white and one that was aqua. This leo was popping, and
with my giraffe ears all perky I was feeling ready to conquer
the world.

When we got to the competition, I ran over to my
friends, the other seven or eight girls on Coach X's team.
All of those times racing my older siblings and having to
fight to be the best would come in handy now. I was going
to *make it* to Disney World! I sat down and proclaimed
excitedly, "I'm going to win this!"

Some of my teammates started crying.

They ran to their parents and told on me. "Jordan just
said *she's* going to win!"

I was so confused. Weren't we all here to win? Shouldn't
they think *they* were going to win too? This was how we
talked in my family. *This* was the spirit of competition—
and we were at a competition, weren't we?

I watched, baffled, as the other girls cried to their parents. Then I saw Coach Dimitri, who was always so nice
to me even as he pushed me to be my very best self as a
gymnast, walk over to my mom in the bleachers and speak
to her. They both looked over at me. My mom had an annoyed look on her face, a look I knew said *are you for real?*
She later told me Dimitri had said he had to come talk to
her about it but didn't really want to. We *needed* that level
of hype and enthusiasm on the team, and he loved that
about me, but he also needed to appease the other parents.

Later, the owner of Naydenov Gymnastics had a meeting with my parents, asking them to make me apologize
to my teammates. The parents had taken it all the way up
the chain, complaining to the gym owner that I'd said I
was going to win. My parents were incredulous. "You want

us to tell her to shut down the very self-motivation that's going to help her win?" They refused to make me apologize. They refused to snatch away my confidence in myself, and I will always appreciate that. What they did tell me was that some people are sensitive and that there's a time and place for everything. Basically, *read the room*. I've always appreciated that too.

This was not the land of trash-talking on the basketball court, as I'd seen my dad and brothers do. That level of enthusiasm clearly did not translate well in the gymnastics world.

But I still won that meet.

I got called up to the podium—*Jordan Chiles!* I got three gold medals and two silver, and I got a plaque that said I'd won the meet and was invited to represent Region 2 in the meet at Disney World. *Oh my gosh, wow!* I thought. This was so much better than just getting a ribbon! I remember thinking, *Wow, I want to feel this way all the time! Disney World, here I come!*

But then I looked around and noticed that Coach X was nowhere in sight. She hadn't seen me get called up to the podium or heard the announcement that I'd won. I frowned, disappointed. I wanted to show my coach how well I was doing.

What she hadn't told my parents beforehand was that she didn't feel the Disney World meet was a worthwhile one for the members of her team, that she wouldn't be traveling to Disney if one of us won—a gymnast needs a coach with them at every meet—and that we shouldn't plan on attending. This was my very first optional meet with Coach X, so we knew none of that.

Before I knew it, one of the judges from this competition came and took my plaque away. Snatched it out of my little eight-year-old hands because Coach X had said that I couldn't go. Tears came to my eyes as I watched that woman walk away with my plaque. Little did I know it wasn't the last time I would be unceremoniously, and unjustly, robbed of something I earned.

My parents, outraged, ended up having an exact replica of that plaque made, and they gave it to me for Christmas, just a couple of weeks later. "You're not about to be robbed of something you earned, Jordan," my mom insisted. That made me feel good, even though I was still upset.

When I look back now, I can't believe the adults at that meet didn't consider the anguish a moment like that could cause me. I was already the only child of color at that meet. And instead of pulling me aside to take the plaque privately, if they had to take it, they'd embarrassed me out in the open and left me there, crying. Later Coach X told me that the Disney meet was beneath me and I should just get over it.

6

FLYING AND FALLING

When I got to level 10, I was only ten years old. Most of the other girls in that level with me were between twelve and eighteen, which was kind of intimidating. And Coach X didn't spend time trying to make *any* of us feel comfortable. Her digs about my hair continued, and I was beginning to understand where they came from. Being on the competition circuit had made me fully aware that my hair was not what the sport was used to or what it was looking for. The other, non-Black girls' hair was slicked back into effortless ponytails or buns, the way Coach X wanted *my* hair to look too—but it simply was not going to work for my kinky, curly locks, and it wasn't what I liked anyway.

Maybe cornrows would be better, my family and I thought. With my hair close against my scalp, what could Coach X possibly say? But when my sister braided my hair into cornrows—oh my gosh, you would have thought my cornrows were going to be the death of everyone. Coach X hated it and remarked about it derogatorily multiple times a day. So I started wearing braids because they were easy to pull up into a more "elite" bun. But Coach X had an even more visceral negative response to the braids. I couldn't believe people didn't see the beauty in my hair the way I did, the way my family did. Their doubt seeped into me, casting a dark cloud over my gymnastics dream.

My parents wanted me to remain authentic to who I was. They wanted me to be proud of myself, of my hair. I couldn't swing it back over my shoulder, like the other girls, and I did not need to. So my parents would do affirmations with me. "What's your name?" they would ask.

"Jordan," I'd answer confidently.

"Right, you're Jordan *Chiles*, and that's the only person you need to be, is Jordan, and only Jordan. You don't need to be anyone else. Is Jordan Chiles enough?"

"Yes," I'd say. "Just being myself, Jordan Chiles, is enough."

But for Coach X, it wasn't.

When she didn't have her eyes trained disapprovingly on my hair, she was inspecting every aspect of my face and body. She told me not to smile because a serious expression looked more focused. I have always had a muscular build, even as a child, but she wanted my shape to change in unrealistic ways to suit her image of what a good gymnast looked like (slender and less obviously muscular, a build traditionally referred to in gymnastics as "graceful"). Gymnastics is a sport of illusion—women gymnasts especially are expected to be powerful without appearing so. The first gymnast I ever admired was Shawn Johnson, the

2008 Olympic balance beam gold medalist and team, all-around, and floor exercise silver medalist. All muscle in an ocean of slim builds, Shawn had a frame very similar to my own. Though I was incredibly young, I'd already spent nearly half my life in intense training, and I knew I looked as strong and powerful as I felt inside. My mother always said I could sneeze and grow muscles! Even without lifting weights, I effortlessly had a more substantial look.

In a sport where coaches often favor the most petite bodies they can find, Shawn Johnson stood out in a way I loved, and I hoped that I could too. She and my other favorites, like Dominique Dawes, gave me permission to be unapologetically strong in a sport that venerates slim white body types, which are often regarded as more feminine and soft, and have historically been seen as delivering the most visually pleasing gymnastic performances. As in sports like ballet and figure skating, the illusion of effortlessness in gymnastics is what has attracted many fans over the years. Fluid movements and long "clean lines," as they're referred to in the sport, are what we are trained to present to the judges. Because of this, the scoring systems have historically rewarded routines performed by more slender gymnasts—and Coach X wanted me to be one of them.

At practices, she constantly called me "bubble butt." *Tuck in that bubble butt and open up those hips, so you'll look more graceful.* I had nearly 0 percent body fat, but she routinely insisted I lose weight and "open my hips wider"—a veiled criticism of my butt, which she thought should be flatter. Even with my hips open as wide as they could go, I still had a butt, as do many Black gymnasts. That's just how we're shaped. Our silhouettes may be curvier than typical white gymnasts', but that doesn't mean our lines aren't "clean." But Coach X would poke at my body and admonish me for putting on weight. "You look like a donut." I started hating my obliques so much—sometimes I still do, if I'm honest—that I once asked a doctor if they could be removed or shaved down.

Most practices began with Coach X asking what I had eaten and done since I'd last seen her. If she felt I'd eaten too much, she would call me names—*frumpy, pudgy*—and give me the cold shoulder. "I know you've gained at least a half pound this week. I can see it all over you," she'd say, before suggesting I stick to clear soups for the coming weeks. "If you were more serious about your career you'd sacrifice more." According to her, coaches around the country could see how much weight I was putting on and were commenting about it to her.

She would even check the food packs that my parents sent with me to practice. Once, my mom had packed an Uncrustables peanut butter and jelly sandwich, and the way Coach X reacted, you would have thought I was swallowing poison. "Gymnasts do not *eat* this!" She thought consuming eight hundred calories a day was ideal, which my parents found insane. They had to cook for a whole family of growing kids, and they weren't about to starve any of us. I remember so many times where I would start eating with my family and then put my fork down. All I could think about was *What would Coach X say?* Her voice would be rattling in my head as my parents made lunch or a snack for me in the morning. "No peanut butter, Dad," I'd say. "That's too much fat. No jelly, Mom. That's too much sugar."

The voice in my head no longer sounded like my own; it sounded like Coach X's. When I looked in the mirror, I'd pinch different areas of my body and feel shame at the way I looked. I became uncomfortable performing in leotards and wearing tight clothes because of the way they hugged my body. Did everyone else see what Coach X saw, that I was fat? Though I was excelling in gymnastics, winning meet after meet, I rarely felt good in my own body.

Eventually, I developed a habit of binge eating. At school, I'd go across the street to get chocolate muffins but then eat healthily at home so that my parents wouldn't know. I felt like I had to hide what I was eating even from them, although I couldn't resist bingeing when I was at family events, tempted by Grandma's table full of enchiladas and tortillas. I never purged after bingeing, I just reduced my calories in the days after, hoping Coach X wouldn't notice I'd consumed more than she thought I should. I was never diagnosed with an eating disorder, but I was wrestling with a very unhealthy relationship with food. I kept the fear and shame I felt to myself. To this day, although I eat what I want, I always feel I need to explain it—as if feeding myself has to be justified.

* * *

In addition to mimicking age-old aesthetic preferences, keeping us gymnasts under a certain weight was supposed to make it easier for us to perform, to soar through the air and get height on our leaps and flips. But the costs were steep. I started noticing that it was completely normalized

for the girls around me to be so thin that they'd stop getting their periods—or wouldn't get their periods at all until
late in adolescence because they were eating so little.

At that time, I didn't yet realize how even the gymnasts I
had always looked up to also struggled with body and self-
esteem issues. We're all so used to being picked apart—for
our performances and our weight—that we get in the habit
of doing it to ourselves.

Shawn Johnson has spoken about severely restricting
what she ate to be in her best shape for the 2008 Olympics, then spiraling when puberty caused her to gain weight
later on. As many female gymnasts get older, men comment more boldly on our bodies and whether we are dat-
able or too "man-like." Black women athletes in all kinds
of sports, like Serena Williams and Caster Semenya, are
often more likely to be deemed "too masculine" than their
non-Black counterparts. That was what I was up against.
As a young girl, I was constantly told—even by the media
and society—that I was too muscular for the opposite sex
to ever find me attractive. I found that terrifying. Being an
athlete didn't stop me from wanting to have a normal social
life, or from caring about what others thought of me.

But, thankfully, my parents already knew that this was
something I'd be up against in life, and they constantly reminded me how beautiful I was and that my muscles made
my gymnastics feats possible. They told me I looked like
a superhero. Yet the more powerful my body became, the
more I shrank from it—and the more critique I was subjected to.

Coach X's constant badgering left my stomach in knots,

and I tried to make myself as small and inconspicuous as possible around her. Part of me questioned whether she was right: maybe I wasn't good enough, thin enough, ambitious enough. I longed for her approval, but I couldn't seem to contort myself into the person she wanted me to be.

7

PUSHED TO THE BRINK

Meanwhile, I'd started noticing that Coach X smelled funny. Sometimes her words would run together, her voice slurring, while we were at practice. She had a water bottle she carried around, constantly taking swigs from it, and she would act weirder and more hostile as the day went on. I didn't know what any of that meant, but what *was* clear was that the better I got at my sport, the more intensely she focused on me above all the other girls. She wanted to know where I was at every moment of my life. What was I doing? Who was I with? She felt that she'd invested a lot of time in me and my potential and didn't want to see it squandered. And I *was* winning meets left and right—but, thanks to her, I seemed to be losing friends at the gym just as quickly.

I once went to a birthday party for one of the other gymnasts, and Coach X called her house to ask if I was there.

How long had I been there? What was I eating? "Don't give her cake! She's too big already, and she needs to be able to compete." Not only was this supremely embarrassing for me, but the other parents started feeling they couldn't even serve cake at their parties if I, Coach X's prized gymnast, was going to be there. My parents started not answering the phone if Coach X called our house when I wasn't home. They didn't want to tell her what I might be up to in my few precious hours of free time. "You can't go to the mall," she would scold me later. "All that walking will give you shin splints!" Being in the marching band at school was a no-no for the same reason. I wanted to play my clarinet and march in the Rose Festival Junior Parade in Portland with my bandmates; when Coach X said I couldn't, I cried and my parents overruled her. I missed practice and she froze me out for the rest of the week.

Desperate to keep tabs on me, she would call other parents when mine didn't pick up. "Is Jordan there at your house? The Chileses aren't answering the phone." The parents would then call my mom: "What do you want me to tell her?" Other gymnasts and their parents started to complain that I was Coach X's pet, not realizing I wanted nothing more than for her to stop fixating on me.

At the gym, she would hold me up as the standard to my teammates. "You see how Jordan did that? You see what she can do? *You* need to be more like her. Work harder! Do better! You're lazy! The only reason you're *anything* is because of me!"

That certainly didn't endear me to anyone. I'd go up to other girls to congratulate them or to ask a question, and they would straight-up walk away from me. It felt like I had nowhere to turn in that gym, the place where I was spending most of the hours of my life. And it was difficult to make friends at school because I was only there for half a day and had no time for school sports or other activities.

As much as I hated when Coach X held me up as an example, I hated even more when she tore me down in front of the other girls—she would swing back and forth between those two extremes. She wrote everything down in one of those spiral flip calendars. She recorded if I skipped training for a school field trip, if I went to a sleepover and woke up the next day and wasn't able to perform well on beam, if I missed a couple of training days because I was sick. She would show me the calendar and say, in front of everyone, "See, this is why you embarrassed me. It's because all these days, here and here and here, you didn't train. You see? You aren't acting like an elite international gymnast. You're lazy. If you're sick it's because you went to your friend's house and to church." Even church was starting to cause friction between her and my parents. "She should be *resting*!" Coach X would insist.

I despised that calendar she was always waving around. And I began to actually dread going to competitions. I knew that if I didn't place first or second, the next few weeks at the gym would be unbearable. I couldn't eat or sleep knowing that Coach X's angry outbursts would take over postmeet practices. I'd lie awake beating her to the punch, tearing myself down in the same way she always did.

Many pro gymnasts train for twenty-five hours per week; I'd been training at least thirty-six hours a week since getting to level 7. Yet if I performed poorly in the eyes of

Coach X—even placing third or fourth—she told anyone with ears that my lack of dedication was to blame. The emotional roller coaster I was on made me inconsistent in front of the judges, despite how capable I knew I was.

*   *   *

My parents could see I was under a lot of pressure. But I didn't tell them the full extent of Coach X's extreme behavior. And Coach X told us over and over that, having trained gold medalists and elite gymnasts in the past, she was the only person who could take me to the next level. "You should be happy that I'm training your daughter because without me, she would be nowhere!" There were no other elite coaches in Region 2 at that time. In fact, that region was not known to turn out elite gymnasts at all. At meets people would whisper among themselves, "Well, you know, nothing good comes out of Region 2," then be surprised by what I could do. I heard it so often that it became a chant in my head, and my parents would remind me of it to keep me focused. "Nothing good comes out of Region 2. That's what people say, Jordan. What are you going to do about that?" Because we were such a competitive family, they knew that I would bite that bait and refocus.

So, when Coach X said these things, that I *needed* her, I believed her. She had always presented herself as the very best, the only one capable of helping me achieve the career I dreamed of. She was my coach, so I trusted her, and I wanted her to feel that I was worth the time and investment she'd put into me. But at the time, I didn't understand the cost of admission.

When we traveled for meets, she was often the only adult chaperone, but she'd show up to the airport acting weird and smelling funny, then rush to the bar as soon as we got through security. She had never been a warm or affectionate person, but the drinking made her more harsh, critical, and mean. Any time I didn't absolutely have to be around her, I'd hide from her. I never told my parents because the behavior felt normal to me, I'd seen it so often. She was the adult. She knew best. And we needed her.

Also, I didn't understand that this was the behavior of someone with a drinking problem, and that it could be dangerous for her to spot and train me in her drunken state. If I underrotated on a flip or missed a release move on bars while traveling alone with Coach X and she was too inebriated to catch me or break my fall, it could end my career or even my life. I just knew being with her was an unpleasant experience. But I could not attend international competitions or National Team camps without a coach, and Coach X was the only one of the coaching duo who traveled. I felt trapped. I could feel my dreams slipping away and it felt like there was nothing I could do about it.

I was walking a delicate balance of putting medals over everything else. I thought, *Maybe these thoughts in my head are fine. Maybe feeling this way is normal, just a part of gymnastics.* There was no price that you could put on my mental health and well-being, but that's what everyone around me seemed to be doing, even me. I was wearing gold medals around my neck, so everything must be fine, I think we all thought. And my parents had never had a kid in gymnastics before; they were trusting Coach X to guide them. But this was getting to be unbearable for me.

And so I started rebelling. Over time, I became more distant and angry. I got to where I couldn't stand to be near Coach X, preferring vault and bars, the events that Dimitri coached, over floor and beam, which Coach X coached me in. She said I had an attitude, but really I was just trying to grasp some control over my situation. "Stinkerbell, you're lazy!" she'd yell. "Work harder!" She'd call my mom and say, "Talk to your daughter. She's disrespectful. She won't look at me when I'm talking to her."

I felt like I was in a dark corner I couldn't get out of. I cried constantly and told anyone who would listen how miserable I was. But my cries were often minimized and dismissed by people who told me that *this* was what it would take to be an Olympian. This is what that hard road most people didn't get to travel looked like. Though they supported me fully and were worried about me, my parents were advised not to pull me out of gymnastics when I was finally so close. I *knew* I was close and I didn't want to give up on that dream. I just wanted the pain to stop.

My mom later told me Coach X had started asking all of the families for weird favors. She would casually say things like, "I'm here training your kid, and I ran out of foundation makeup. Can you run to the mall and buy this for me?" At the time, I didn't know that this was going on, and I was completely shocked to hear it. But this sort of behavior created strange bonds between Coach X and the parents of the kids she was coaching. So many of the parents at Naydenov absolutely loved her because they thought she could get their kids college scholarships or maybe even onto an elite track. They were also afraid of her, but my mom was not. My mom often resisted Coach X's asks. "I need to stay here and train the kids. Would you go buy me some thong underwear from Victoria's Secret?" No, my mom told her. That was inappropriate. And yet Coach X's habit of asking favors created an informal vibe that, on the right day, might *almost* feel like friendship. My mom now says that she, like all the parents, was definitely getting played.

As time went on, I wasn't the only one who had noticed Coach X's distinctive odor. "You can smell it coming through her pores!" I overheard my mom tell my dad. "She came into the gym drunk, or from last night drunk, smelling like that?" Sometimes she would even miss practice altogether, and it would be Dimitri holding down the fort until she returned. My parents reported her behavior to the gym owner, and for a while she seemed less erratic. But then one night, Coach X called my mom, drunk, from Portland, just across the bridge from Vancouver, where we lived. "I need help, I need help!" she slurred.

My mom got in her car and drove across the bridge to pick her up. She found Coach X drunk, completely toasted, at a street festival. It was only nine at night, and she was already hammered. My mom took her home. As they sat in the car outside of her house, Coach X admitted that she had a drinking problem.

"Okay, well, are you ready to fix it?" my mom pressed. "Because the coaching doesn't even matter at this point. Your life does. You need to get your life together, X." Despite everything, Coach X was a lost soul, and my parents were pastors. She was also their kid's coach, someone who functioned as my chaperone, guardian, and coach all rolled into one when on the road. They couldn't turn a blind eye and not help her. And they hoped against hope that her drinking was the cause of all the cruelties she inflicted—if they could just get her to stop, everything would improve.

My mom helped her get into a rehab facility. Coach X was away from the gym for weeks, while I continued to train under Dimitri. None of the other families knew that she was gone because she was in rehab—I didn't know either; I simply accepted whatever excuse had been given and breathed a sigh of relief that I'd have some time away from her.

When she came out, she wasn't as mean or as fierce as she had been; she was slightly more relaxed. But if we thought the changes would last, we would soon find out otherwise.

*   *   *

When I was still just ten, I had attracted the attention of the USAG National Team staff and all of the college coaches, and I started getting full-ride scholarship offers from colleges around this time. Every college you can think of with a gymnastics program, I got an offer from. (I was the number one recruited gymnast of my class, and, by seventh grade, I'd verbally committed to attending UCLA.)

"Oh, we did it, baby!" my mom recalls Coach X saying as she swaggered up to her after that first Nationals meet that garnered me so much attention.

"What are you talking about?" my mom asked.

"The National Team staff wants Jordan," Coach X replied. "She's been invited to their camp."

The National Team camp was an invite-only opportunity for gymnasts to compete and train among the best of the best. There are eleven of these training camps a year. Being invited to National Team camp doesn't mean that you've automatically made the National Team, but it does mean that they see potential in you and want to see where that potential can go. This was the next step I needed to take toward my dream of making it to the Olympics. Beaten down though I was, I was starting to feel as if my dream *could* one day be real.

*   *   *

I wore tree braids to National Team camp in Texas—small, individual braids that allow your hair to be free-flowing on the ends. It was a style that I could easily pull up into a ponytail or a bun, while keeping my own hair protected from heat or damage. I was so used to Jazmin doing my styling that I hadn't really learned how to comb or grease my own hair yet, so the braids made it easy for me to manage on my own while I was away from home.

I was now twelve, and Coach X accompanied me to the camp in Texas as my coach and chaperone. She was carrying that water bottle around again, but I didn't think anything of it. I stayed in the hotel room with her the day before camp started. (This was before Larry Nassar had been convicted of sexually assaulting dozens of female gymnasts in his role as the USAG team doctor, so there weren't the same rules governing accommodations for gymnasts and adult chaperones as there are today.) In the hotel room, Coach X looked at me with disgust. "Jordan, this hair—it looks terrible. This isn't the elite international look." She shook her head and ushered me into the bathroom. "Come, look."

I looked in the mirror and saw my freshly braided hair. The braids fell to my shoulders. It looked great to me. I looked like my normal self, so I didn't know what she was talking about. But she left the room and came back with a pair of scissors. "I'm going to make you look better."

And before I knew it, she took that pair of scissors to my hair. *Chop, chop, snip.* The ends of my braids fell to the bathroom floor. My eyes welled up. But I was too afraid of her to tell her to stop. So I just stood there as she cut not just the braids, which were extensions, but also my real hair.

Afterward, I called my mother from my cell phone, in tears. There was a pile of my hair on the bathroom floor, and my mother was miles away in Washington. Protection and safety felt so out of reach. I was trying to be quiet as I called her, so Coach X wouldn't hear, but I was sobbing. I must have been completely incoherent. I was trying to say everything all at once, to express how horrified and humiliated I was even as I sobbed.

"What!" My mother was completely outraged, telling me over and over again as I pressed my ear to the phone, sniffling: "Don't listen to her, Jordan. Oh my gosh, I can't believe she did that! Your hair is beautiful. *You* are beautiful! The way that you're made is beautiful. Everything about you. Your skin color and your hair are gorgeous. Did you say anything to her when she started to cut your hair? Did you say no?"

"No," I cried. "I didn't say anything. I didn't know what to say."

Then my mom said, "Let me speak to her."

I went to get Coach X, gave her the phone, and walked away, tears rolling down my cheeks.

"I made her look better" was the first thing Coach X said into the phone.

"You do not touch my baby's hair!" I heard my mother yell. "You do not touch someone else's hair, much less a Black girl's hair! You have no idea what her hair means to her! And you didn't even know what you were doing. You just used random scissors. You just hacked away at my baby's hair!"

"You should be thanking me," Coach X responded simply. She was completely unfazed and hung up the phone soon after. I never got an apology.

Now I was more terrified of Coach X than ever. Calling me "bubble butt" and "two heads" and "sack of potatoes" was one thing, but this made me feel utterly silenced.

I couldn't have put it into words, but her continual focus on my hair—and the aggression she had just used in attempting to make it conform to her wishes—encapsulated so much about my life in gymnastics. How do you become what you've never seen? From the moment I began seriously training, I rarely saw other Black gymnasts, and I never saw Black people as authority figures in the sport. For so many years, I don't recall seeing a Black coach or trainer and very few team doctors. I've never seen a Black judge, the people who are judging and scoring our body positions—or on our selection committees or in high-ranking positions within USA Gymnastics. Because of this, I often found myself surrounded by preconceived notions of who I was and what I could do—how much I could achieve and how good I could be. I wanted to defend myself against their preconceived notions of me, but having to always feel and be on guard was exhausting. At the same time, I felt I had even more to prove.

Over time I would realize that most Black gymnasts come up against something similar, and hair often plays a role. I once competed with Gabby Douglas at an international competition (the 2016 City of Jesolo Trophy) and got to see how talented she was up close. But at the same time, online and across social media, most of the mentions about her were about her *hair*—which she often wore pulled back and gelled up into ponytails and buns—not her *talent*, and these critiques came from Black as much as non-Black people. Years later, Gabby opened up about how the pressure to assimilate within gymnastics had destroyed her natural hair, leaving her with bald spots from the tension and products that didn't work well on her textured hair.

I knew that hair is a statement that a lot of people have taken away from them, whether for political or assimilation reasons. And I refused to go down without a fight. I continued to wear Afro puffs and allowed my hair to be an extension of my personality in gymnastics, as I still do today.

And not long after I got home, my mom gave me some advice to help me stay strong through tough challenges. "Scripture could help you really believe in yourself and feel like you can do all things—like you can just go out there and succeed and do everything that you need to do within your life," she said. "You should remember Philippians 4:13 . . . 'I can do all things through Christ who strengthens me.'"

I nodded. *You know what,* I thought, *this scripture is going to be with me every step of the way.* And it has been. "That's my scripture," I told her. "I'm going to take it with me. I'm going to use that motto. I'm going to use that as much as I can and really believe it."

As I became an elite gymnast, I was subject to the world of drug testing. I've been drug tested since I was eleven years old. As athletes, we have to tell the United States Anti-Doping Agency (USADA) where we're going to be every hour of the day—that's how serious the testing is. If a rep shows up randomly to test you, you'd better be where you said you were going to be. Even if I went to spend the night at someone's house, my family had to update them.

Drug testing is supposed to be randomized, but I've always felt over-tested. Being Black and at the top of your game means there will always be officials and fans who believe that it can't just be my natural ability or evidence of my hard work that makes me do well at gymnastics—like the women my mom overheard when I was a child who thought I must be using illegal enhancement drugs like steroids. To them, it's unfathomable that I could be naturally talented and achieving such feats without the help of drugs. At the same time, white athletes who actually *do* use drugs—including tennis, track and field, and gymnastics pros—can go undetected for years. I'm always shocked whenever a new doping scandal arises. How were they not caught for so many years, when I was once tested three times in a *month*?

The lack of transparency around drug testing makes it hard to tell if some groups are truly more scrutinized than others. But the fact remains that competitors and spectators often express skepticism that Black athletes are succeeding on talent alone. Add to that, women athletes need to be twice as good for half the recognition, so being Black *and* being a woman makes things that much harder. And in a sport like gymnastics, which values whiteness and strength while demanding women gymnasts look more dainty than powerful, Black women need to be *three* times as good to counter all the strikes against us.

But this level of bullying often leads to long-term body dysmorphia and low self-esteem for young gymnasts like me. Male athletes are expected to be and look strong, while girls and women are encouraged to be lean and elegant despite the immense amount of force needed to perform the moves we do. I have found that the unrealistic expectations and opinions people have about gymnasts' bodies stem from a lack of understanding of how difficult it is to do what we do. We've all heard of naturally athletic people who can bounce between sports, from football to baseball, track and field to soccer—but no one, athlete or not, can perform a vault or swing between uneven bars without first having *years* of very specialized training. What we do as gymnasts is often underappreciated because part of the skill is to make it look easy—and this is the case for Black female gymnasts most of all.

8

BILES AND CHILES

first met Simone Biles, the woman who would one day become my best friend and sister in gymnastics, in 2014. I was thirteen and she was seventeen. I had made the National Team the year before, after becoming, at age eleven, one of nine girls in the country to qualify for Junior International Elite. As a Junior Elite, I was on track for competing at international competitions, and I was training at an elite level. And at that time there was no camp more elite than the Károlyi Ranch National Team Training Center in Huntsville, Texas. We all just called it the Ranch.

Owned by Béla and Márta Károlyi, Romanian coaches who had defected to the US and opened their own gym, the Ranch was where women's National Team gymnasts and Olympians trained. On the fifteen-hundred-acre property outside Houston were cows and peacocks, deer, horses, and even camels. In addition to the Károlyis' home and the gym where we all trained, there was also a sleeping quarters for gymnasts. No parents were allowed on the premises.

I loved seeing my friends at the Ranch, but the conditions there were awful. We lived in cabins that smelled like sewage and were infested with bugs. It could have been like camping—but I've done camping before, and this was not it. They never gave us enough food because they were always trying to keep us from gaining weight. One time, my friends and I snuck into the cafeteria and stole some Pringles because we were so hungry. We had powdered eggs for breakfast, and since there were peacocks all around the grounds we decided we were probably eating peacock some days—that's how bad the food tasted. There were times when I cried in the shower, wishing I could go home.

But it would have been hard to get out of there. The Ranch was in such a remote location, down a long dirt road on a compound in the middle of the Texas forest. *If a helicopter tried to come and save us, where would it even land?* we used to wonder. There wasn't immediate access to hospitals, so there was a team doctor on staff. That doctor was Larry Nassar. Many of the sexual abuses that later sent him to prison took place at the Ranch, which would close in 2018 after the Károlyis were hit with at least a dozen civil lawsuits related to the Nassar scandal. He was my doctor that first summer (I was there for three), and I noticed he liked being extra friendly and giving us candy. But I was not one of the many he abused back then, when no one knew of his assaults and the Ranch was still the go-to gym for elite gymnasts.

When I met Simone there, I was starting to make waves in the gymnastics community. I was at the Ranch with

Coach X (who had been coached years before by Márta Károlyi), training for my international debut at the 2014 City of Jesolo Trophy, an annual women's gymnastics competition in Jesolo, Italy. (There, I would win a gold medal with the team and finish sixth in the all-around.) Simone hadn't yet competed in her first Olympics, but she was already becoming a big name, certainly in gymnastics circles, and I was starstruck.

I had seen Simone around the compound, but we were always training with our coaches and never really got to speak. Then one day several of us gymnasts ended up hanging out and talking at the end of a long day. I nervously said hi to Simone and told her, "I'm a huge fan. Like, you're one of my idols." She seemed flattered but responded humbly. We chatted a little more with the other girls, and then that was it.

In August, Simone and I separately headed to Chicago to compete at the US Classics. She was a senior and a big deal; I was just a junior, new on the scene and not one of the young "it-girls" expected to make a splash in the junior competitions. It was my first big national meet, but my parents and I thought I had a real shot at finishing in the top ten of the junior division, which would have made us all over-the-moon happy.

And then something amazing happened. I performed in the morning, along with some of the other juniors— the ones expected to do better would be performing that night. But I scored so well that after my session, as my family and I left the gym for something to eat, spectators were waiting outside cheering and asking me for my autograph! Part of me wondered if they had me confused with someone else. I couldn't believe it. I stood there signing autographs for little kids and their parents for a good half hour—it was crazy. And that night, after the rest of the juniors and all of the seniors had competed, Simone took the senior title and my score held: I won the US Classic in the junior division. Biles and Chiles! The media couldn't resist that rhyme, and luckily Simone and I would soon build a friendship that made us feel like an actual team. There's a picture of us hugging after the competitions, at the hotel where we were both staying. Every time I see it I think, that's where it began. Biles and Chiles was meant to be.

*   *   *

Simone and I had more in common, of course, than rhyming last names. Simone's rise had come with renewed grumblings in the gymnastics community about the differences between Black and white gymnasts, and I was now old enough to really pay attention to how this affected our sport. In 2013, shortly before I first met Simone, she performed a new skill that had never been successfully completed at a world or Olympic competition because of its difficulty. The move was named after her in the Code of Points: the Biles (Floor), a double layout with a half twist in the second flip. (She has since created and successfully performed four other gymnastics moves that have been named after her.) With the arrival of increasingly difficult moves, the gymnastics scoring system had to adjust to keep up—the maximum difficulty score available for our routines rose. This meant that athletes who were unable to perform these skills at this level felt they were now at a scoring disadvantage.

In 2016, after Simone became the first Black gymnast to win an all-around world title, with the Biles (Floor) named after her, Italian gymnast Carlotta Ferlito told her teammate Vanessa Ferrari, "Next time we should also paint our skin black, so then we could win too." (Both had competed in the 2016 Olympics but neither had medaled.) When Ferlito's comment became public, her coach defended her and followed up with his own racist take: "Why aren't there Blacks in swimming? Because the sport doesn't suit their physical characteristics. Is gymnastics becoming the same thing, to the point of wanting to be colored?"

When Valeri Liukin, a celebrated Kazakh-American gymnast and coach and father of Olympic medalist Nastia Liukin, was asked in 2019 about the success of Black gymnasts like Gabby Douglas and Simone Biles, he had some strong words as his response. He stated that the scoring systems had now changed to favor "power" over "grace"—a change he interpreted as giving Black gymnasts an edge. "In the Code of Points, difficulty is very valued now. Of course, this suits African Americans. They're very explosive—look at the NBA, who's playing and jumping there?" This man was the coordinator for the United States women's national gymnastics team, from September 2016 to February 2018, replacing Márta Károlyi. Apparently, it wasn't that we were talented athletes who'd excelled in the sport, raising the bar and setting new standards for everyone else to keep up with. Even those in charge of our sport held these biased views of us.

The added layer of social media—which gymnasts in the

past didn't have to navigate—has only increased the hatred often directed at Black gymnasts from enthusiasts who wish for the days when the sport looked different (that is, whiter) than it is today. What follows is a random selection of social media harassment directed at various Black gymnasts:

She looks homeless.

She doesn't deserve that medal.

What big arms and hands and a huge neck you have.

Artistry in women's gymnastics died when Nastia retired sadly! The sport is now ugly looking! ZERO beauty, it's all acrobatics! I so miss the 80s, 90s & early 2000s era.

Long slender limbs are elegant. Thicc is not.

Little did I know how all of this would shape my mental health journey over the next two Olympic cycles.

9

BREAKING POINTS

One night in September 2016, my parents were watching the local news at home in Vancouver when a story came on that struck fear into their hearts. A former gymnast named Rachael Denhollander had accused Larry Nassar, the team doctor for USAG since 1996, of sexually abusing her. Larry Nassar: the doctor at the world-renowned Ranch, where I had spent three days training just months ago. My parents were stunned into silence—and then the texts and emails from other parents started pouring in. How had families not been made aware of this privately, before the world was told? Had Nassar abused other girls? Were their own daughters safe?

I was asleep in my bedroom at the time, and my mom and dad agonized over whether to wake me. My dad was in favor of talking to me in the morning when I was rested and could really understand, but my mom couldn't stand not knowing if I'd been a victim. I remember being nudged out of dreamland to see them standing over me, asking questions I couldn't wrap my mind around and telling me I hadn't done anything wrong. What were they talking about? I knew I hadn't. Could I please just go back to sleep?

As my grogginess lifted, I slowly absorbed the horrible news. I was in shock. But Larry Nassar had never touched me inappropriately, I reassured them. In the ensuing weeks and months, the scandal broadened. We learned that the doctor so many young gymnasts had trusted had sexually abused hundreds of girls, including my teammate and mentor Aly Raisman. My parents questioned me again and again about every interaction I had had with Nassar. It seemed clear that he had begun grooming me. I recalled him being extra friendly and giving me, as well as other girls, candy and other treats. We were so underfed at the Ranch that goodies were a sure way to our hearts. My mom remembered seeing his "nasty little hands," as she put it with a shudder, on my leg one day after I'd injured my knee. He'd told my parents, "I'm gonna need her to come and see me." And he had DMed me on a Facebook account she had access to, congratulating me on doing well in competitions.

My mom now thinks that, in a terrible irony, Coach X's obsession with me made it difficult for him to get me alone. Even at the Ranch, she rarely let me out of her sight. We counted ourselves lucky, even as our hearts broke for the girls he had so brutally violated. I was traumatized and I felt helpless that there was nothing I could do. I refused to hear that monstrous man's name spoken or the topic addressed, and I became more and more withdrawn.

My life with Coach X, meanwhile, was getting worse by

the week. In October 2016, she accompanied me to national training camp at the Ranch. There had been a leadership change at USAG—just before the Nassar scandal exploded into the media Márta Károlyi had retired. The Károlyis had transformed women's gymnastics: before their leadership, the US women had never won Olympic gold. By the time Márta retired, we had become the "dominant force," as ESPN once put it, in women's gymnastics. But it was time for new blood at the top of USAG. By the time I arrived at national training camp that fall, Rhonda Faehn and Valeri Liukin were in charge.

Throughout the three-day camp, Coach X was acting erratically. She would yell at people, she would cry—I remember her throwing her shoes at practice. When she wasn't looking I took the top off of her ever-present Starbucks cup and sniffed it: straight alcohol.

One day she left me unattended during a practice, which is completely against the rules. Rhonda Faehn was paying attention. Later that day she pulled me aside. "Jordan, if you ever feel unsafe around Coach X, use the word 'pineapple' and we'll remove you," Rhonda said. She'd given me a safe word.

"Huh?" I had no idea what she was talking about.

When I got home I told my mom that Coach X had been acting like a weirdo. Worried, my mom contacted Rhonda, who said she'd reprimanded Coach X for leaving me unattended. Rhonda also said she'd smelled alcohol on Coach X's breath one day at camp, but when confronted Coach X said it was just mouthwash. After my mom and Rhonda talked, my coach was essentially put on probation: she was no longer allowed to drive me to and from camp, and if her unacceptable behavior continued, she would be out. My parents were reassured by those measures and wanted to believe Coach X's mouthwash story, but they had more than a few doubts.

After camp ended Coach X stayed away from the gym for three days, refusing to train anyone. My mom and I saw it as punishment for our family's questioning and reporting of her. It was not the first time she'd done this when she was angry. There had been complaints about her over the years from families and gymnasts who'd had negative experiences at national meets and camps, and she'd received multiple written warnings from USAG, although with little follow-through. But many of the other parents at Naydenov saw her as the messiah who could help their kids win. So when she would leave for these punishing stints, they would write her notes—*You're so amazing, Coach X! We miss you!*—groveling for her return. They eyed me with disdain because they knew we had complained.

And they were already angry at us. All the publicity for the gym that was now coming in was because of me—like the Audi commercial and Disney's *Citizen Kid* segment I did when I was thirteen—and the media was saying I was poised to be the next Gabby Douglas. The other families seemed to think, *Coach X isn't paying attention to us anymore. Our kids don't matter to her; only Jordan does.*

*   *   *

I was now a teenager, fifteen years old, and trying to find my own voice. I was heading into my first year as a Senior International Elite, after being a Junior International Elite from ages eleven to fifteen. You're considered a Senior International Elite beginning in the full year that includes your sixteenth birthday. That's when things get big, allowing gymnasts to qualify for the World Championships and the Olympics, and I was right on the cusp of it. But the walls of darkness felt like they were closing in on me faster and faster, and I didn't know where to turn.

"What do *you* want?" my parents would ask me. "What is your dream? Because everything you have told us is that you want to be an Olympian. Only you get to choose if and when you want to quit. Don't give anyone that power over you."

The thing was, I didn't know the answer to this question anymore. I felt like I didn't know *anything* for myself anymore. So I started trying to write about it. Maybe if I could just get my thoughts down on paper, they would make more sense to me.

In the little bit of downtime I had, I'd sit up in my room and pull a sheet of paper from a notebook. I would stare at that sheet of paper for what felt like hours. The pen would hover shakily over the paper. Finally, I'd take a deep breath and just let it all fall out of me, what I was feeling at that moment. Then, with finality, I'd nod, take another deep breath, and fold the note into fourths. On the way to school in the morning, I'd leave the note on the kitchen counter, propped up against a canister or teepee'd and with *Mom* scrawled across it, for my mom to find before she went to work.

I left her these notes several times, and they would always say something like this:

I don't want anything to do with this sport anymore. And I know what you're going to tell me. You're going to tell me that I need to remember what my dream is. But I don't want this dream anymore. I don't want anything to do with it anymore.

Gymnastics and Coach X had become intertwined, and my love for gymnastics was now gone. The first time I wrote one of those notes, I didn't know what her reaction would be. All day at school, I thought about it. *What will she say? Is this really the end of gymnastics for me?* But when she picked me up after gymnastics that day, she was patient and sympathetic. We didn't say much during the car ride, but when we got home, she parked her SUV in the driveway and then didn't unlock the doors. This was her method with us kids. When we parked in the driveway and she wouldn't unlock the doors, we knew that a long and serious talk was coming.

I turned to face her, steeling myself. *What will she say?*

"Mom, I don't want to talk about this right now."

"Jordan, I think you do want to talk about it. That's why you left me that note." She paused and let this sink in, then continued, "My job here isn't to talk you out of anything. I just want you to remember, what do you want?"

Slowly but surely, my words came. Letting all of those words out—confused and jumbled as they may have been—seemed to help. Letting out my frustrations seemed to help.

My mom told me she'd recently seen an interview with Nastia Liukin, who retired in 2012. "Nastia said her mom used to tell her, when she would have a bad or frustrating day at the gym or competition, 'You can quit on a good day, but not today. If you have a good day at competition or at the gym, and you *still* want to quit, then you can quit *that* day.' So I'll tell you the same, Jordan. Today is a bad day. But if you still feel this way after a good day, then you can quit. At least then we'll know you won't have any regrets. I don't want you to quit because of your coach or your friends or whatever. I want it to be because it came directly from you and not from your frustration. So just use Coach X as a tool to get where you're going, and don't let her stop your dreams."

We talked for what seemed like an hour, just sitting there in our car in the driveway. My mom let me decide for myself that I wasn't going to let this woman stop my dream. I was closer than I'd ever been before, nearly the age that FIG, the International Gymnastics Federation, would allow me to compete in the Olympics if I could qualify— and I couldn't let Coach X prevent that, not after all that I'd already been through.

"Now, who are you?" she asked me before she would let me out of the car.

I said it with pride: "I'm Jordan Chiles."

*   *   *

With Larry Nassar gone, Coach X and I traveled back to the Ranch so that I could train for the 2017 City of Jesolo Trophy after having done so well there in 2014 and 2016 as a Junior Elite. In 2015, Simone had swept every event except for the uneven bars. I hadn't attended that year. I got sick during the verification process and had to be isolated from the other gymnasts so that I wouldn't get them sick as well. I completed my verification process after recovering from my illness, but Márta Károlyi, who was very,

very strict, had decided not to put me on the 2015 team to, quote, "teach her to want it more." Like Coach X, Márta believed that getting sick was no reason not to train. But this year, I felt I had a good shot at being selected to compete there again.

At the Ranch that year, Coach X would be gone for stints while I was training. We later found out that on one such occasion, she'd asked another coach to drive her into town, saying she needed to go to the pharmacy. He did so, thinking nothing of it, but was then concerned when, on the way back to camp, he heard glass bottles clinking in her bag. He later reported it to Rhonda and Valeri.

At the end of the training camp, my mom got a call from Coach X. She was slurring. "They didn't pick Jordan," she said, sounding inebriated. "They didn't pick her because she's Black." She was making up whatever she could to keep the focus off her—although maybe the alcohol had loosened her tongue and she knew more than we realized.

"Wait, wait, Coach X"—my mom stopped her incoherent ramble—"are you drunk? Why do you sound drunk?"

"No, I'm not!"

"How could you be drunk right now, Coach X?" She was supposedly sober but my mom could already hear it in her voice and was livid. "How could you be drunk, when training camp just got done?"

Coach X kept slurring, protesting that she wasn't drunk, but then my mom saw a call from Huntsville, Texas, coming up on the other line. "Coach X, I have to go," my mom told her, disgusted. "Someone's calling on the other line." It turned out to be Rhonda and Valeri.

"We have some really bad news," they told her. Then

the truth came out. They told my mom that Coach X was absolutely intoxicated right then, no question. She'd gone into the dance room at the Ranch training camp and told all the girls in the room that they "sucked" and "you don't know how to dance!" Then she proceeded to sway drunkenly around the room. The other female gymnasts there were uncomfortable and embarrassed for me. They called her crazy. They did not feel safe in her presence. She had been filling her water bottles and her Starbucks cup with vodka and drinking while coaching at the Ranch.

"What! I thought she stopped drinking!" My mother was furious. But this was a new regime in charge, and they'd let her know as soon as they found out—an improvement over the last regime.

They told my mom that Coach X was being banned from the National Team and all National Team activities. "We're very, very sorry, but the reason Jordan didn't make the Jesolo team this year is because we can't send her without a coach, and Coach X will not be able to travel with the team." So I was unable to compete at the 2017 City of Jesolo Trophy, but the real reason was never disclosed to the public, presumably because it would have made USA Gymnastics look bad—and they were already in the midst of the Nassar scandal. Once again, instead of furthering my dreams, Coach X's behavior was holding me back.

Rhonda said they weren't going to tell Coach X she'd been banned until after she had gotten me home safely. Who knew how she might try to take it out on me? Rhonda wanted to protect me, and my mom was so grateful.

I still didn't know, at the time of that call, that any of this was happening.

Still, no one would tell me exactly what was going on. But they did tell me, later that day, that I hadn't been selected for the 2017 Jesolo team. I was crushed. I had done so well this entire year, and also at the selection camp. Maybe I hadn't trained enough this year. Maybe I hadn't shown them that I was worthy of competing as a senior this time, rather than as a junior.

The next day, Coach X and I were set to fly home to Vancouver. "You don't train like an International Elite," Coach X spat. "I told you what happens when you're lazy!" As I cried to myself, those words repeated over and over in my head. *You're lazy!* Maybe Coach X had been right all along.

When we got to LAX for our layover from Bush Intercontinental Airport in Houston, I sat at one of the gates, waiting for our flight back home, and sobbed. What had I done wrong? Self-doubt flooded through me like a wave, drowning me in negative thoughts.

I tried to bury myself in my phone, flipping through apps to take my mind off it. Instagram. Pinterest. When I looked up a bit later, I noticed that Coach X was gone. *Wait, what?* I stayed there for a while but finally went looking for her, walking from gate to gate, my backpack in tow. Had she just left me there at LAX?

Finally, I called my mom.

"Ummmm, Mom, I can't find Coach X," I said as soon as she answered.

"What!?"

"Yeah, we're at LAX, but she's gone. I don't see her anywhere. I think our flight is out of another terminal. How do I take the shuttle to find it?"

My mom was immediately frantic, but I felt oddly calm. Too much had happened to me to be easily rattled anymore. If I could just find my way to the next terminal, I'd get on the flight myself and be fine. But then, as I walked through the airport, I saw Coach X sitting at a bar.

"Oh, there she is," I told my mom. "She's at the bar."

"At the bar?!" My mom was absolutely spitting mad, but I was too exhausted to process any of that. I hadn't been chosen for Jesolo, and I was starting to feel like my sport just didn't want me anymore.

I went over to Coach X and told her we needed to go. She looked blurry-eyed. The pieces were starting to fall into place for me—that she didn't just drink sometimes; she had a problem. I just wanted to get back to Vancouver, to my own home, my own bed, to think and process things. Luckily I didn't have to sit next to Coach X on the plane. If we sat together she would say rude things to me the entire flight, so we had a team parent who always sneakily moved my seat reservation to a different part of the plane. I'd pretend to be clueless when Coach X asked why we weren't together.

When we landed in Vancouver, my mom was there waiting for me. She hugged me so tight you would have thought I'd had a near-death experience. I remember her asking over and over again if I was all right. She turned to look over her shoulder at Coach X, shaking her head at her.

In the car, my mom teared up. She pulled into our driveway and threw the car into park but didn't open the door. Again I knew that this was going to be one of our talks, but I didn't expect what came next.

"I need to talk to you about something," she said. "We—we've been keeping things from you, your daddy and I. Because, well, because you were too young to understand and we didn't want you to feel too much pressure. But the thing I want you to know right now"—she took my hand—"is that it's not your fault that you didn't get picked for Jesolo. It's not your fault. You didn't do *anything* wrong at camp, do you hear me? Nothing."

And then she told me what had happened, the phone calls she'd received the day before, that Coach X was going to be banned, that it wasn't my fault I hadn't gotten chosen.

And I bawled.

"I thought *I* did something wrong," I cried, nearly incoherently. "I thought I was doing things wrong, and she let me believe it. She let me believe that the reason I hadn't gotten picked for Jesolo was because I wasn't good enough!"

"I'm so sorry, Jordan. I'm so, *so* sorry," my mom cried. She explained the other things she hadn't told me—about the severity of Coach X's alcohol problem, about having sent her to rehab. "Never will I ever allow you to be in that kind of situation again." And those words hit me so hard. There was so much I hadn't told her either—like the fact that I'd been seeing Coach X at airport bars regularly for years, and that she'd asked me to take the wheel and drive her places even though I didn't have a license (and I'd complied). We'd been shielding each other, until this very moment when the truth came out.

But my mom didn't let me take any blame. "I should never have let it get this far," she said tearfully. "Whether it was because of Coach X's manipulation or me wanting you to finally achieve your dream—that she could bring you success—I should have never thought the way she's so hard on you was normal. I failed to protect you, and I am so, so sorry for that."

I leaned into my mom and let her hold me. I knew that she had always been in my corner. I'd never heard her say *I'm sorry* so many times in a single conversation, and I knew that she was hurting too. I couldn't be angry at Mom or my family. It was Coach X who had tried to make me believe that I was less than I was.

"This sport has not been kind to you, Jordan," my mom said. "And you've given it your all. So if you want to walk away right now, let's go. I'm with you, and we'll just walk away from this." I nodded, processing her words, trying to hold them in my head as I wiped my tears. "But if you want to continue, it's not going to be with her."

At those words, I could feel my face light up. Like warm rays of sunshine were hitting me after being in darkness for so long. I had never really considered life and gymnastics without Coach X, because she was *the best*. She was *the only one who could*. But the thought of never having to see her again lifted such an emotional weight from my shoulders. "Whatever you decide to do—continue gymnastics, go on to college at UCLA, whatever—you're going to excel at it. Gymnastics is not who you are, it's what you do, and you're going to be amazing at whatever you decide to do."

I took in every single word she said. I was done crying now, and her words gave me such resolve and determination.

"No," I told her. "This is what I want to do. I believe in myself, and I'm *not* going to give up. *She's* not going to be the reason I give up on my dream of becoming an Olympian. If I leave this sport, it'll be on my own terms. If I leave this sport, I'll leave it on a good day."

My mom smiled through her tears and squeezed my hand. A year later, she would submit testimony to a Senate committee on preventing abuse in athletics. She would tell them about Coach X's behavior during that training camp—an important step toward ensuring that no other gymnast would go through what I had.

But for now, I was just relieved that Coach X was finally out of my life. I could breathe again.

10

A NEW PATH

In the weeks that followed, the light began filtering back in. I no longer felt like I was in a dark corner where no one could reach me; I felt my own voice coming back and strengthening in my head. More and more, it was not my cruel coach's words that I heard in my mind but my own. I started to feel like my old self—and my gymnastics skills became more consistent.

But I also realized that Coach X wasn't the only hurdle I had to overcome in gymnastics. My sport was still largely white, rigid, and racist. And I still needed to find a new coach who could train me at an elite level, a feat I knew would be hard in Region 2. Dimitri could still train me on vault and bars, but I needed an elite coach to train me on beam and floor, as well as someone who could take me to competitions since Dimitri didn't like to travel. This would be a tall order to fill in my region, where there were only a handful of coaches with any level of elite training experience.

We asked around with other gymnastics families and found Coach Tiffany, a woman who came highly recommended. Despite the fact that she had never trained an elite gymnast before, she *did* have experience coaching in all four events. After being under the elite wing of Coach X, with the high expectations she'd drilled into me over the years, I knew this was going to be a big adjustment for me—and for Coach Tiffany, who would be in the bright lights of the global gymnastics stage for the first time.

I was feeling optimistic about the upcoming 2017 US National Championships and World Championships training camp for team selection after that. I'd still never made a Worlds Team. But, as I was training for Nationals, Coach Tiffany was personally told by Valeri Liukin that I should only train one vault. Traditionally, gymnasts who excel at vault perform two vaults from "different families," since you can't medal in vault without doing two. (The vault families are categorized according to the different ways a gymnast can approach the vaulting table, called "the entry.") The two scores are then averaged together for your final vault score. Vault had always been my strongest event, and I was planning to do an Amanar—a difficult vault that includes two and a half twists in the air, something I'd been performing for years. I'd also been training a Lopez as my second vault, a half-turn entry front layout with a half twist. I was confident that the Lopez could help me finally secure a spot on the Worlds Team because it would prove I had medal potential.

My mom and I complained to the coaches. This seemed

crazy, and not right. I needed to perform *two* vaults. But our voices went unheard because Tiffany was new and didn't have a voice at the National Team level. "Well, let's just get this Amanar perfect first," I was told.

Valeri Liukin was the same man who had publicly stated that the changes in scoring systems unfairly advantaged Black gymnasts' "power" over the "grace" he thought was important, discounting our skills and contributions to the sport. As USA Gymnastics' National Team coordinator for the women's program, taking over after Márta Károlyi stepped down, he held much of the power and influence in gymnastics at the time. His word was often the final say, and his opinion was highly regarded throughout the sport, both nationally and internationally. It felt as if he was trying to hold me back when he held me to unrealistic standards that no one else was held to, like trying to stick an Amanar. And the entire time that I was at National Team camp, he made remarks that I should open my hips more, just as Coach X had always done because she thought that would make my butt look flatter and my "lines" cleaner. I was worried and unhappy under this biased kind of scrutiny I thought I'd left behind when I parted ways with Coach X, but Valeri reassured Coach Tiffany and me that I was "completely in consideration for the all-around" at Worlds and that performing a second vault wasn't required for me to be considered for the team.

Our decision to walk away from Coach X, who was now banned, had stirred up a lot of whispers among other gymnasts and their coaches. How would I perform now? Would I be even more inconsistent in my performances than I had been before? Would not having Coach X in my life mean the end of my gymnastics career? What could this mean for them and their chances of making it onto the Nationals and Worlds Teams? But, at US Nationals, I finished in second place, taking silver at only my second Senior Elite competition and shaking the gymnastics internet after an unconventional save on beam.

Beam has always been my arch nemesis—my least consistent event. That night it was my last rotation, so I was pretty tired. As I was executing something called the wolf turn—basically a squat turn with one leg extended out on the beam—my balance was off and I tried to steady myself by . . . standing up. Which is literally crazy; you just don't do that. I still had my spinning momentum so I ended up doing a triple turn on top of the squat turn. The audience kind of gasped and I heard afterward that the commentators were in complete shock, like *I don't know what she just did there, it's basically impossible! If someone tried to replicate that a million times they wouldn't be able to pull it off.* I was pretty surprised myself, and even more surprised when the judges gave me a really high score. People started calling that move the "wolfkino" after that—a combination of the wolf turn and the "okino," a triple turn named after '90s gymnast Betty Okino.

I felt more confident walking into Worlds Team camp after winning that silver, and once there the reactions around me told me that I was beating expectations of how I would perform without Coach X. Before the Worlds Team had even been announced, other coaches who were there were DMing and texting me and my parents their congratulations. After seeing me at camp, they felt there was no way I wouldn't make the team.

Only the all-around winner at Worlds Team camp automatically secures a place on the Worlds Team. The next three spots and one alternate are selected by committee. USAG heads are not part of the selection committee, but it's long been the unspoken way that their influence is paramount there. That was the case when Márta Károlyi was the head of USAG, and it was the case now, with Valeri Liukin in that role. The same Valeri Liukin who had been criticizing me and had told me not to perform a second vault.

Still, I and other gymnasts and coaches at Worlds Team camp were convinced my performance was strong enough for me to make the 2017 team. But when the selection committee announced the team, I was named as a non-traveling alternate. I would not even be traveling with the team, but would be on non-traveling reserve. They'd selected a gymnast with an injury instead of me, supposedly because she already had international experience. She was a phenomenal talent, but I was surprised that an injured gymnast had been chosen ahead of me. It felt like a punch right to the stomach. I couldn't understand why I hadn't made the core team, until I was told that not performing a second vault at Nationals and Worlds Team camp had severely hurt my chances of being selected, even though I'd placed second overall. A decision that my parents and I had railed against from the start had now proven to be the downfall to making the 2017 Worlds Team. Tiffany was shocked—even after she'd told Dimitri to stop training me on the Lopez, she had gone back and asked again and again if I could do two vaults, and I'd actually finally started training for the Lopez in 2016. But Valeri continued to insist I didn't need it.

Making the Worlds Team was supposed to be my proclamation to the world that I was back and better than ever, as I bounced back from the traumas of my time with Coach X. But, instead, it was just another blow to my self-esteem. For years, I'd been missing out on opportunities because of Coach X and her behavior, but now, it was internal politics that I was up against. It did make me feel better to go online and see the outcry on Facebook, Reddit, and Twitter criticizing the decision, but those words of affirmation couldn't fully ease the sting.

My gymnastics career has been filled with slights, slurs, microaggressions, and derailments. And now it was becoming harder and harder to hide my true feelings about it. At times I felt numb, at other times the pain burned right through me. Finishing up 2017 and going into 2018, I kept smiling and performing through my suffering and anguish, but inside, I was slowly breaking down. There were a lot of things going through my brain. When I think about it, I just wanted to take my own life. I didn't say anything to anyone about this, but I felt it. Like *I don't wanna be here anymore. I just don't wanna be on this earth.* I thought this more than once. Deep down, I knew there was more to me; I wasn't going to do that to myself. But when I think back on 2018, what I went through was very much like a death.

One day that year, I glanced around my bedroom, giving all of my trophies and medals, ribbons and plaques a good long look—and I felt no emotion at all toward them. In fact, I wanted to pack them all up and toss them in the trash. Just the sight of those awards made me sick, after years of all I'd had to suffer to earn them.

"Please, Mom, just get *rid* of them!" I said. "I don't care; dump it, burn it. I just don't want to see this stuff anymore!"

I didn't want friends who came over to see them and start asking all about them. I was sick of the sport, sick of feeling unwanted and unappreciated within it. *You know what*, I thought to myself, *if no one wants me, then what's the point of me continuing?* Being snubbed for a spot at Worlds felt like the last straw.

But, again, I wrote my mom a note and left it for her to find. And, again, I decided that I should quit on a good day, not a bad one.

Yet those thoughts had already taken root in my mind, and I started mentally checking out of the sport. By this time, I was sixteen and able to drive myself to practice in a car my parents and uncle had gotten me for my sixteenth birthday. But I stopped going to practice. I'd tell my mom that I was heading there but then would go to the mall or get my nails done instead. After years of watching what I ate, I started eating candy and springing for Starbucks. I started going to my friends' birthday parties and sleepovers and other social events, after years of often skipping fun things for fear of what Coach X would say. I didn't get a boyfriend, exactly, but there was a guy I liked a lot and got to hang out with. Romantic relationships were pretty much off the table since I spent so much time training— and that's a problem that continues to this day. I fall asleep at ten p.m.! Even though I'd been dreaming of love since I was eleven or twelve. I used to wait until my dad was out of the country, then text him to ask, "Can I have a boyfriend now?" I knew he told my sisters they could have boyfriends but not until they were forty-two! So I was too scared to ask him in person. "You can have one when you can explain to me why you need one," he would always reply. I didn't know why I needed one, I just knew I wanted one, so we didn't get very far.

Now that I was in my mid-teens I needed time away from gymnastics—maybe not for dating quite yet, but for normal socializing. I wasn't yet sure of how to say that to my parents with finality. So I just kept pretending to go to practice, skipping frequently, while living my life on my own terms.

*   *   *

That following year, my performance was clearly suffering. When I headed to the 2018 US National Championships, things looked glamorous and people cheered me on, but, internally, I was fighting that darkness. I was very depressed. *What is the point of even being here? Why am I competing? I don't want to.* There were just a lot of things going on inside my head that were not okay. I think a part of me was just out there trying to show America—and maybe myself—that I was not a quitter. But deep down, my heart was shred into pieces. I felt like I was in a tunnel. Like I was in a box and there was that one little crack that has a little light, but I could never reach it. Every time I reached for it, it got further away. Every direction I turned, there was just blackness. There was nothing beautiful about what was happening within me.

But on the outside, your girl looked bomb. My leos were fire—my mom and I were designing them ourselves since we'd left Coach X. In my hair, makeup, and sparkly lilac leo,

I looked as good as all get out, even as, inside, I felt like an ant. Like a zombie. I had never felt so bland and blank in my brain. I was so devastated and disappointed. But these emotions were a sign of weakness, according to Coach X's voice in my head. I needed to have my game face on 24/7.

Through day one of the competition, I tried to shut out the noise in my head and just focus on each event, one by one, as I headed into them. I scored a *15.000* on my first event, vault, with a beautifully executed Amanar. I felt good about that score and that performance, but I couldn't beat back the anxiety in the next events; my leaps and landings were off on beam and floor. On day two, I traded my lilac leotard for a Wonder Woman–inspired one. For my floor routine, I'd chosen the theme from the new Wonder Woman movie with Gal Gadot, and my mom had the idea of designing a leo to go with it. Even as low as I felt, I couldn't wait to show it off that day. Gymnastics is so rigid and strict—about how our hair and bodies look, what we wear, what music we choose—and that leo definitely went against what most people would choose. It vibed cosplay more than elite gymnastics, and we even threw in little touches from Wonder Woman's Black sister Nubia, who's powerfully built just like me. Rules are rules, but I was saying, *This is who I am and the world's going to have to accept it.*

If I'm honest, that leo made me feel more powerful on the outside than I did within. My floor score went up slightly while my vault and beam performances suffered. I'd taken one step forward and two steps back. At the end of day two of the 2018 US National Championships, I finished eleventh in the all-around competition. I felt there was no way I'd make the National Team that year.

I felt utterly disappointed in myself. I remember telling my parents, "I failed, I failed." On the way to the car afterward, I was sobbing as my dad kept his arms tight around me. In my head I was thinking, "Maybe my career is over. I don't want to do this anymore—there's nothing for me to give anymore. This dream is over."

But my mom knew just what I needed. She could see that I was feeling low, not at all like who she knew me to be, so she and my dad decided to gather all of my favorite people together for a trip to my favorite place on Earth: Disney World. "We need to get her away from gymnastics," my mom told my family. "Let's go!"

The day we were getting ready to leave, Coach Dimitri had a conversation with my mom that took her by surprise. He told her, as he had before, that I was very gifted, but this time he added that if I wanted to make it to the Olympics I should probably switch to a gym with more elite athletes. As much as he selfishly wanted to keep me, he thought moving was what I needed. I was shocked when she told me. It was so kind and selfless of him. Even though I couldn't imagine leaving Dimitri—the coach who had kept me sane and alive in the midst of Coach X's mistreatment—his words did get me thinking.

But even that incredible vote of confidence didn't lift me out of my depression. Neither did a shout-out from Gal Gadot (aka Wonder Woman) herself. She had reposted my routine, which made it go viral even faster than it already had been. But I couldn't reconcile all of the positive things people were saying about me online with how I felt about myself inside. I simply didn't believe all of these positive words could be true. That I was *amazing* and *inspirational*, *so talented* and *the one to look out for*. For what felt like forever, I'd been trained to beat myself down whenever I had a less-than-stellar performance. I could hear Coach X's disgust in my head again, after not living with that burden for so long.

My parents, siblings, aunt, uncles, and grandparents—sixteen of us in total—were spending a weekend at the happiest place on Earth, and I couldn't shake off my despondency. "Forget about gymnastics," my mom told me. Then she stood by as I followed her instructions and removed all my social media apps from my phone. I really tried my best to hear what she was saying, to internalize the affirmations that were coming my way, but my inner voice had learned to be utterly brutal and knew exactly how to beat me down.

*   *   *

A couple of weeks later, I was named to the National Team at Worlds Team camp. My mom kept reminding me how impressive that was. I'd been named to National Teams for four years in a row. But after two back-to-back competitions that hadn't gone as I'd hoped, I couldn't stop questioning whether I should quit the sport anyway.

Simone and I had been in more constant communication at this point, and we'd had a few conversations over the years in which we were both candid about what gymnastics had taken from us. In January 2018, she had tweeted a message that would be heard around the world with lasting repercussions in our sport: "It is impossibly difficult to relive these experiences and it breaks my heart even more to think that as I work toward my dream of competing in Tokyo 2020, I will have to continually return to the same training facility where I was abused." She was talking about the Ranch. I was shocked and devastated for her. She had never before revealed that she was one of Nassar's victims. I respected her privacy and didn't ask her about it: we still haven't discussed it—not once. It's a trigger for her and something we've taken out of our vocabulary.

Three days after Simone's tweet, USAG ordered the Ranch permanently closed and cut all ties with the Károlyis.

*　　*　　*

After US Nationals, ten to fourteen elite gymnasts are selected to attend Worlds Team camp depending on how well they did at Nationals, giving you the opportunity to show your skills to get selected for the Worlds Team. Simone and I, now twenty-one and seventeen, were both selected for the camp, which—with the Ranch now closed—was in Sarasota in late 2018. There, I talked with her again about the rough road I'd been on during my gymnastics career and the mental health struggles it had caused. I told her I was seriously questioning if gymnastics was for me anymore, even as I was literally at the Worlds Team camp, surrounded by my gymnastics peers and the apparatuses I'd been flipping on for nearly my entire life.

"Yo, I don't know what to do," I told her. "I don't know if I can continue doing this."

She had noticed I wasn't performing like my normal self. It must have been obvious to her that I hadn't been training as much. But she was like, "You know, you have the talent,

Jordan. You have the gift. If you want to do it, do it. And if you don't, then don't. But I think you should really focus on the fact that you have the ability to make the Olympic Games." I was so close, she reminded me; even in that very moment, we were at camp for Worlds, an accomplishment in itself. I was too close to quit now.

I think I would have given up if it weren't for that life-changing conversation and what she said next.

"Look, if you've gotta switch coaches or gyms, then you just gotta switch," she advised me. "You can come to the World Champions Centre"—where she trained, in Texas—"and see how you like it, if you want."

She understood the pressure I was up against better than anyone else. She had been subject to even higher levels of scrutiny and violence at the hands of adults she'd been told to trust. When Simone encouraged me, giving me what I'd been missing for so long in gymnastics—empathy and a chance at a new beginning—I felt something reignite within me, even though I didn't get selected to the Worlds Team that year. But I didn't feel like I was at the level I needed to be to get selected, anyway, after the rough year I'd had emotionally and my lack of training for several months.

That unexpected suggestion from Simone immediately felt like it could be the solution to the mental, emotional, and logistical training snags I'd been up against. It could solve all of my problems at once, providing me with the coach I needed to support and train me at an elite level. The World Champions Centre (WCC) had two exceptional coaches, Cécile Canqueteau-Landi and Laurent Landi, who'd trained Olympic gymnasts before. Maybe this could actually work.

Moving to WCC wouldn't be as simple as just signing on a dotted line. I still lived in Washington and was in my senior year of high school. A move to Texas would be an enormous change for me, taking me away from the only home I'd ever really known. But graduation was just a few months away, in the spring of 2019. The timing seemed perfect. *Maybe, before heading off to college, I could put one last effort into elite gymnastics,* I thought to myself. I was formally committed to attending UCLA, but maybe I could defer. Maybe I could give Olympic-level gymnastics one last shot, for real.

I never make major life decisions without consulting my mom and dad. My next conversation needed to be with them. Honestly, I was so nervous—terrified, really—to bring such a big ask to my parents, so I decided to ask them when I knew they'd be distracted. This year, I knew, was especially hectic because a property in Portland that my mom ran as a wedding venue was being filmed for *The Great Christmas Light Fight* on ABC. It was an old Victorian house my parents decorated with tons of lights every year, and this time we were doing it bigger than we ever had before because we would be nationally televised. We had sixty-foot-tall candy cane trees, and the entire property was lit up, from the trees to the walkways to the two-story house itself. You could probably see it from outer space.

So, of course, I felt this was the perfect time to spring my pitch. People bustling around, looking at the light displays. I pushed through the crowds, making a beeline toward my mom and dad. They had created a little store on the property to sell holiday items like ornaments and lights. Yes, they definitely looked busy enough to be distracted by my crazy ask. They were fielding questions from this person and that. Maybe they'd be too preoccupied to ask too many questions, to find flaws in my plan.

"Mom, Dad, I need to ask you something," I said.

"What? Right *now?*"

"Yes, it's super important!" I insisted. Then I just let it tumble out: "I want to keep going for the Olympics. But . . . it can't be here. I need to move."

For me, everything stopped right then. All I could focus on was what they would say. But, to my surprise, they laid my fears to rest immediately and were in complete support of me. They had been there for me as I'd struggled through the past couple of years, been firsthand witnesses to my mental health struggles with the sport. They'd seen my deep depression. In that moment, my dad told me something I've always held on to: "We have supported every one of our kids' dreams to the fullest, and we don't intend on stopping now. So, if you feel like you need this, then we'll figure out how to make it happen."

We spent a week doing research about the various other gyms that might work for me, but Texas came out on top. I didn't want to disrupt everyone's lives, and I thought I was all grown up—I could move by myself. But my parents had their limits. The plan: I would stay in Vancouver to graduate with my class in June 2019 (which wasn't ideal with the Olympic year right around the corner, but I really wanted that bit of normalcy). I would defer my acceptance to UCLA and my mom and I would move to Texas; my dad and siblings would visit often. My journey to the Tokyo Olympic Games had begun.

11

LEAN ON ME

To close out my senior year in high school, I went to prom in a red sequined mermaid dress, played along on senior skip day, and got locked into the school with my classmates for a fun night of senior festivities—all things that would have been unthinkable under Coach X. Things that most elite gymnasts never do, especially the year before an Olympics they hope to be a contender for. That's also around the time I got my first tattoo, the word *Blessed* on my left forearm. My parents had always told me that I'd have to wait until I was an adult to get a tattoo—they weren't really about that life and didn't approve of me having one before I turned eighteen. So as soon as I became an adult, I went and got that first one. I've since had to have it covered up because the workmanship just wasn't great, but that started my love for tattoos. I now have about two dozen. When people ask me about them, I don't even know where to begin; I have so many and they all mean something to me.

I have a rose over that original tattoo, and another rose I got later, behind my ear. I love roses. They're so beautiful, and my grandma Yvonne, my mom's mother, had planted an Olympiad rose bush in her backyard, telling people, "My granddaughter's going to go to the Olympics," before I even went. She had that much belief in me. I also had my birth flower, the daisy, tattooed underneath my left arm, and then a separate tattoo with the words *little sunshine* to remind me of my childhood days when my mom would sing me, *You are my sunshine, my only sunshine . . .*

I would later get a tattoo of the galaxy, because I've always been amazed by the stars and planets. I also have the number *23*, Michael Jordan's number, and a line drawing of two faces that reminds me of beauty, like how you look in the mirror and you see the beauty in everybody and yourself. That tattoo reminds me, *You're beautiful. You're elegant. You have the ability to embrace yourself.* I also have *pray* on my hand. Before each competition, I pray with my hands together. I was like, *Well, I might as well get "pray" on my hands.* It gives, *Okay, this is what I've always done ever since I was little.* And I have butterflies tattooed on me because I've been a nature girl ever since I was little.

Two of my favorite tattoos are sayings and scripture: *Everything happens for a reason*, a life model that I've told myself since leaving Coach X, and my go-to, *Philippians 4:13.* Then I also got *God is greater than all highs and lows* and *Your grace is sufficient for me* on my back. A cross on my wrist. Koi fish on my spine to remind me of my love of the natural world and the serenity that can be found there. (My parents built a koi pond in our backyard when I was around fifteen or sixteen.) *Divine* on my thumb because my sister Jazmin's health and beauty company is called J. Divine, and that word reminds me of her. *Angel* on the back of my arm. A half circle of olive leaves on my sternum. *Patience* on my hands. Roman numeral *V* on my ear to signify my position in the family as the fifth child. Three of my siblings also have their Roman numerals tatted.

But back to my last days of high school: I just wanted to be a regular kid and experience all the things that young people my age were doing. I'd been denied those experiences for too long, and I had a blast just getting to be a high schooler. Two days after graduation, I headed for the June national training camp, then moved to Spring, Texas, and walked in the front door of Simone's gym.

Within weeks of being in Texas, I knew that God had guided me to the right place. Coaches Cécile and Laurent were the supportive figures I'd been searching for all along. Soon after I arrived, Cécile told me she had never met such a gifted athlete who thought so little of herself. I wanted to see what everyone else saw. For so long, I'd been battered by the world, and it had eroded my trust in anyone outside of my core circle. At WCC, I finally felt seen and valued by coaches who wanted to encourage me to be my full self within the sport, bringing out the best in me rather than trying to force me to fit a preconceived mold. There were even other girls there who looked like me, so not only was I no longer the star athlete of the gym, with the pluses and minuses that entailed, but I also no longer felt like I had to overcome my skin color and hair texture in the gym. WCC had gymnasts from all ethnicities and walks of life.

The entire atmosphere at WCC was a much-needed shift for me, a true leveling up. As the baby of my family, I'd always felt the benefit of having older siblings, and Simone seemed to step into that role for me seamlessly. She became a big sister to me, someone who knew exactly the physical and mental hurdles I'd been up against. Through her friendship, so much of my heart had begun to heal. I was training alongside her and other gymnasts who were experienced and skilled enough to challenge me to new heights.

I have often said that Cécile and Laurent are the dopest people I've ever met, and I mean every word of that. They have always been truly genuine in their concern for and support of me as a human being, not just a gymnast. I know that they truly wish the best for me, both in and out of the gym, and they gently pushed me to be my fullest self in my sport while helping to rebuild my confidence that had been torn down over the years.

Under their guidance, I started to find my love for gymnastics again. Now when my mom asked me my name, I answered with joy and pride: Jordan Chiles.

And the world began to notice. Because I'd delayed moving until I graduated from high school, I was now on a very short timetable to prepare myself for the Olympic Trials. The road to the Olympics passes through four major competitions: the US Classic, the US Championships, the World Championships, and then the Olympic Trials. I went to Classics after I'd been training with Laurent and Cécile for only a few weeks, and to Championships a couple of weeks later. I competed in all four events at both and finished well, and the media noted how happy I suddenly looked. I was dancing, laughing, and hyping up the crowd. That's what calms my nerves, and my new coaches learned that very quickly and encouraged me to be myself, instead of staying rigid and inexpressive, which is what Coach X had insisted on. She thought engaging with the crowd made it look as if I wasn't paying attention. My parents tell me that now, if they don't see me dancing when I'm out there on the floor, they know there's something wrong.

I didn't make Worlds in September, which was gutting for me, but my coaches kept me focused on my longterm goal: the Olympics. For once I was surrounded by supporters who wanted to build me up, not critics bent on tearing me down.

*   *   *

The rest of 2019 held more challenges than I would have liked. A persistent discomfort in my wrist had been diagnosed as a torn ligament that needed surgery—not what you want to hear heading into the Olympic year. I was told to allow six weeks for healing, and I devoted myself to conditioning without using my hands. It took more like ten weeks before I had full range of motion in that wrist, and by then I was so tired of just conditioning and modified training. Then COVID hit, and our gym shut down in early March of 2020. We started doing zoom trainings involving strength and conditioning exercises. We crossed our fingers amid the rumors that the Tokyo Olympics would be postponed. On March 24, the announcement came: the Olympics would not be happening in July as planned.

*　　*　　*

On my nineteenth birthday, in April, Simone threw me a little party at the house where she lived. Sitting in the kitchen with her sister Adria, Simone and I talked about this new reality and what our paths forward would be. "What are we going to do?" Simone asked me. She had committed to going through 2020, but a whole additional year was a lot. She had won Olympic gold and multiple World Championship titles at this point, and every time she stepped onto the competition floor, people expected perfection. That weight of expectation, she admitted, was crushing.

I was still unsure about my own road. You work your entire life for the Olympics, and then in the moment when you're eligible, the world shuts down. "I could still just go to UCLA," I said. "I want to make the Olympic team so bad, but I just don't know . . ."

I had already deferred a year at UCLA to make a run for the 2020 Olympics, and when I talked to one of the coaches about a possible second deferral, he told me, "You have a 99.9 percent chance of not making it into school if you don't come now." So there was a lot weighing on my mind about which direction I should choose now that everything would be delayed. As the conversation continued, I found myself fighting back tears. Simone was too. We admitted to each other that there was still more we both wanted to accomplish in gymnastics, but we were determined not to let it ruin our mental health.

"Are we in this together?" I asked Simone. "Because if we're gonna do this, we're gonna go for it."

We looked at each other.

"I'm down if you're down," she replied. "Let's do this and see where it takes us."

We hugged and Adria said, "Yay! We're doing the Olympics!"

I laughed. "Yes, we are!"

That night, Simone and I committed to giving it one more shot. In that moment, it was no longer about walking away with any specific medal. It was about competing in a way that felt most authentic to us, and not losing ourselves in the process. We just had to make sure we were both okay.

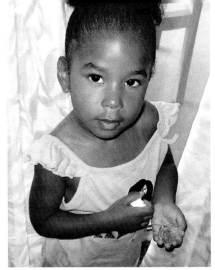

Going for the silver . . . This is me at three, holding some quarters I found while helping my sisters clean our rooms. My mom says I was like, *I found them, I'm keeping them.*

I was seven here, competing at my first level 4 meet. Look at that focus—you can tell I had learned about judging and scores by then.

FAR RIGHT: One of our coaches, Joy Rethaford, giving me a pep talk before I get on the beam at a level 5 meet later that year.

In 2008, a friend of my mom's photographed me and my teammates in white tank tops and jeans instead of leos. She wanted to show us looking as strong and tough as gymnasts really are.

I loved wearing my hair in "giraffe ears" for competing. Here I've just won the all-around at a level 7 meet in 2008 and gotten a trophy, which was *so* much better than plain old medals.

Seven-year-old me after winning my first full sweep—making the podium for every event at a meet. It was at Great Wolf Lodge in Grand Mound, Washington, and I'd told myself I'd get to go to the water park there if I won. I was always reward-motivated!

I won the Rock-and-Roll classic at my home gym in 2008. That year I chose The Jackson 5's "I Want You Back" as my floor routine music.

Tiny ten-year-old me can't hide my excitement as I head to my very first national team camp. It was an honor to be chosen to attend, especially at such a young age.

When gold medalist Shawn Johnson came to Portland after the 2008 Olympics, I waited in line to get her autograph. I wore my favorite sweatshirt and the hoops I begged my parents for because they reminded me of the Olympic rings.

Here I am at national team camp, at ten or eleven. My coach during those years was so hard on me, but my passion for my sport kept me going.

In eighth grade I marched and played the clarinet in Portland's Junior Rose Festival parade, despite my coach's warning that marching would give me shin splints (it didn't).

Biles and Chiles! Simone and me after the 2014 U.S. Classic. The day before, she'd told an interviewer that I was her favorite junior gymnast—we didn't know each other very well yet, and I couldn't believe my ears.

Dreaming I'd make it to the Olympics myself one day, I lobbied my parents hard for this Team USA jacket in 2012. I wore it to the team's show when their post-Games tour came to Portland.

I was in a restaurant after the 2014 U.S. Championships when Olympic medalist Dominique Dawes walked in. Another pinch-me moment: when I went over and introduced myself she said, "I know who you are, Jordan!"

Displaying my medals—and my braces—at the 2014 National Championships. I was so excited about those braces, mainly because of the colored rubber bands. I loved matching them with my leotards.

At the 2016 City of Jesolo competition in Italy, Gabby Douglas won the senior title and I won the junior. *From left:* Gabby Douglas, me, Emma Malabuyo, Aly Raisman, Gabby Perea, Ragan Smith. CREDIT: ALESSANDRO GAMBERI

A family Disney World visit (*from left:* Jade, Jazmin, Mom, Dad, me) in 2014. I love all the rides, including the scariest roller coasters. When I was too young and small to go on them it made me so mad.

In 2018 my sister Jazmin realized her dream of owning her own hair salon. We all gathered to celebrate the opening: (*clockwise from left*) my brothers Taj and Ty, Jazmin, me, my sister Jade, Dad, and Mom.

I'm the gymnast, but my sisters Jade (*left*) and Jazmin (*right*) leaped as high as I did at Disney World in 2018. Maybe that's because it's our favorite place on earth.

In 2019 I signed the NLI— National Letter of Intent— saying I'd accepted an athletic scholarship to UCLA, my dream school. I had wanted to go there since childhood.

Not another picture, Mom! We were trying to organize my medals and figure out how to display them after we moved to Texas in 2019.

This was right before my final year at Prairie High School in Vancouver. I felt so grown up wearing my Senior shirt.

They tell us gymnasts not to wear heels—you could twist your ankle, or worse. But I love them, and I went all out for my high school graduation in 2019.

Simone and I at the airport, dressed in travel casual, en route to a competition in 2019. We often show up coincidentally wearing the same clothes but in different colors.

I had just climbed up a wall to get a hug from my dad after the 2021 U.S. Championships. Being in his arms is my comfort place.

Four Black girls from the same gym in Texas (WCC) made the Olympic trials in 2021, which is pretty incredible. That's Simone and me on the left and Zoe Miller and Amari Drayton on the right.

Biles and Chiles in Tokyo, 2021. It was still mid-pandemic, but we were hoping to achieve our Olympic dreams.

Simone and I pose after podium training at the Tokyo Olympics in 2021 with our coaches Cecile and Laurent. We had to put our masks back on right after this.

Team USA feeling strong, ready, and grateful to be there after podium training. *From left:* Suni Lee, Simone Biles, me, Jade Carey.

CREDIT: CECILE LANDI

After the Tokyo Olympics we headed to New York City for a media tour. It was fun, but Simone and I were eager to go home to our families.

Vancouver threw a parade for me after the 2021 Olympics. It was so cool to see my city come together to celebrate me. They even gave me the keys to the city. CREDIT: SHAWNTE SIMS

Looking at the tattoo I got to honor my Grandpa Gene helps ground me. The words are something he always said: "Where you are I have been, where I am you will be."

CREDIT: ELIZABETH CONLEY/*Houston Chronicle*

During my freshman year at UCLA, in 2021, kids would sometimes show up to meets asking for my autograph. I was happy to do for them what my gymnastics idols had done for me.

My dad trying to breathe some encouragement into me after an NCAA meet in Utah in 2021. It was my freshman year, and although I was doing well, we were struggling as a team.

For my 2023 NCAA floor routines, I chose a compilation of '90s hip-hop. You can see from my face how happy it made me.
CREDIT: KATHARINE LOTZE

This was the end-of-season gymnastics celebration at UCLA in 2023. I had done well, but I'd decided to defer the next academic year to pursue my dream of making it to the 2024 Olympics.

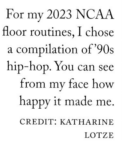

I don't try to hide my feelings on the floor anymore. I knew I'd just nailed this vault at a meet in 2023. CREDIT: KATHARINE LOTZE

I'm no stranger to Paris—I won these medals at the Paris World Cup in 2022. It was at the Bercy Arena, where the Olympic gymnastic competitions were held two years later, so I felt right at home.

Back at UCLA in 2022, my World Championship and Olympic medals and I posed for team pictures.

CREDIT: JESUS RAMIREZ/ UCLA ATHLETICS

LEFT: At World selection camp for 2022, they let parents come down to the floor and greet us, which isn't always the case. We all felt confident I'd done well, but you can never be sure.

LEFT: At the Essence Fest in 2022, I was invited to speak on a panel about Black women's experiences in professional sports.

CREDIT: ERIKA GOLDRING

In an interview I did in 2022, I opened up for the first time about the emotional abuse I'd been subjected to as a young gymnast. Transparency is the only way to make sure the girls who come after me in the sport are safe.

Kayla DiCello and I grab a moment to relax in our official team warmups before the Pan Am games in 2023.

I was the most experienced member of the team at those Pan Am games, so I was the de facto leader—giving everyone permission to be themselves. *From left:* Tiana Sumanasekera, me, Zoe Miller, and Coach Cecile.

Coach Cecile stands proud with the three WCC athletes who'd made the team that year: Tiana, Zoe, and me.

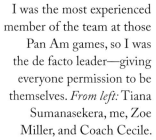

Cecile and I at the opening ceremonies, where I was named a flag bearer. I represented all Team USA athletes at the 2023 Pan Am games, not just the gymnasts—a huge honor.

My coach Cecile is like a second mother to me. Here she is telling me how proud she is at the Paris Olympic Trials.

Carrying each other—that's what friends are for! Simone and I strike one of our favorite poses after the 2024 Olympic Trials.

After the 2024 team had been announced and the confetti had fallen, the five of us took a selfie to immortalize the moment. *Back row:* Suni Lee, Hezly Rivera, Jade Carey. *Front row:* Simone, me.

When they announced the 2024 Olympic gymnastics team members in Minneapolis, they called my name first. I came out and just dropped to my knees, overcome with gratitude.

I've always loved making snow angels, so I decided to lie down and make one in the middle of the confetti. Why not?

NBC asked some prospective Olympians to do promo shoots in 2024—and then surprised us with billboards of ourselves. I'm giving "fours up," which means "Let's go Bruins"—a shout-out to UCLA.

JORD
CHIL
Gymna

#OUTFRONTPRIME

PARIS
NEXT SU

To: Jordan Chiles
Congrats to you Queen, pride and admiration!
I always watch you with
Thank you
for
reppin
us.
Good Luck
to you!
All of your
hard work
and
sacrifice
shines
Bright
Praying for you and wishing you the Best
love your twin
Beyoncé

Beyoncé sent me this personally inscribed album right before I left for the Olympics. When I opened the box, I screamed with shock and joy.

Simone and I after a training session at the Paris Olympics. We like to put socks on to keep our feet warm between routines.

PARIS
2024

Feeling confident after podium training in Paris, I struck my favorite pose: peace signs with tongue out.

I felt good after bars in Paris qualifications too. And that leo with the stars was one of my favorites. CREDIT: JOHN CHENG

I call him Uncle Snoop! Snoop Dogg sat next to my mom and dad and really got into the action at the Paris qualifications.

CREDIT: © WALLY SKALIJ/GETTY IMAGES

My support group turned out in force at the Paris trials. *Top row from left*: my Grandma Yvonne, my Grandpa Ted, a friend, my Grandma Pam, my Auntie April. *Bottom row from left*: Dad, Mom, my Uncle Joe, Jazmin, Jade, Ty.

A dream come true: Simone cheers me on as I leap into my coach Cecile's arms after learning the score on my floor routine had been adjusted and I'd won bronze.

CREDIT: © MEDIANEWS GROUP/PASADENA STAR-NEWS/GETTY IMAGES

Simone and I bowed to Rebeca Andrade, who won gold, on the podium—the first all-Black podium in Olympic women's gymnastics. We knew how much hard work she had put in and we wanted to acknowledge her. CREDIT: © ELSA/GETTY IMAGES

Gold and bronze! We were told there's a tiny piece of the Eiffel Tower inside each of the medals we won in Paris. CREDIT: JOHN CHENG

You've just medaled at the Paris Olympics—where will you go next? Disneyland Paris, of course! My family and I went for a celebration day. It's smaller than Disney World (my fave), but still great.

Happy days in Paris. This was after the Games, but I actually compete with those long nails. They make me even more careful about staying technically sound in my routines.

I'm getting to be a pro at interviewing, and at speaking out on issues I care about. Here I am at my family's dining room table in Texas, making my voice heard. It's a good feeling.

You can tell which one's the gymnast by the box she's standing on. . . . At a Danone sponsorship featuring powerful women in sports, with sprinter Sha'Carri Richardson (*center*) and soccer star Kristie Mewis (*left*).

After the bronze medal was taken from me, Flavor Flav presented me with a bronze clock at the VMAs, where I was a presenter. It was completely unscripted, and I was surprised and overwhelmed with gratitude.

CREDIT: © KEVIN MAZUR/GETTY IMAGES

I'm holding my bronze medal as I look toward heaven on August 5, 2024, silently thanking God and dedicating the medal to Auntie Crystal and Grandpa Gene. I wouldn't be where I am without any of them. CREDIT: JOHN CHENG

12

TOKYO BOUND

The postponement of the Olympics due to COVID-19 gave us more time to prepare. What had been set to be a whirlwind training experience now offered me additional weeks to get settled into my new training facility, my new routine in a new state, and the idea of really going for this dream of the Olympics. It also gave me the kind of time I'd never had to slow down, to sit with my thoughts. It's not lost on me that those benefits came during the pandemic, a period of so much pain and loss, but that was my experience.

I suddenly wanted more ways to convey what I was feeling, and I started getting artistic and inspired in new areas, especially through drawing. At first, I started sketching things randomly. It took me back to a time when I was little and I used to draw with my uncle. We would draw Pooh and Piglet back then, and now I started back down that same path. I remember drawing an elf ear once, then a pair of jeans with lips on them—random things that made me feel good, that act of just getting whatever I was thinking in my head onto paper. I bought myself a sketchbook and pencils, pens and paints. Being an elite gymnast had, in some ways, already started making me a figure for public consumption, and I'd been trained all my life how to perform for judges, but drawing gave me a feeling of calm and an outlet for self-exploration that was just for me.

But the clock was ticking even as the pandemic months seemed to just float along. And the immensity of what I was aiming for was always in the back of my mind. When the gym opened back up in May, I was worried I would have lost my skills, but it was the opposite. My body and mind had fully healed, and for the next several months heading into the Olympic year I was feeling better than ever.

In February 2021, I won the all-around at the Winter Cup. It was the first major gymnastics competition since COVID had started, and that win gave me a major boost. But I was starting to have bad practices—days where I couldn't do a dismount, or my landings were messy. Gymnastics is such a mental sport, and I was putting too much pressure on myself. Simone kept reminding me, "It's going to be hard, it's going to be hard, it's going to be hard. But you just have to keep your mind in the right setting, on the right path, and you'll be good." My friendship with her helped. She reminded me of who I was and what I was capable of, and she was vulnerable enough with me to open up so that I would know I wasn't alone. She too had had rough patches, physically, mentally, and emotionally.

My coaches were frustrated that I could perform beautifully one day and not the next. They still had faith in me, and I was beyond grateful for them. Only one coach is allowed to accompany each athlete to the Olympic Games, and if Simone and I both made it, Laurent *and* Cécile could go. Cécile had never coached at an Olympic Games, and I would have done anything to make that happen for her—which supercharged my stress.

One day during a rough training session at the gym, when I'd been beating myself up for not performing well, Simone's mother, Nellie Biles, noticed signs in me that she'd seen before in her own daughter. As soon as my mom walked in the door to pick me up, Mrs. Biles pulled her aside in the lobby of WCC and said that she was concerned for me. She said that Simone had struggled in similar ways around the time of the Rio Olympics in 2016; once we get so close to our goal of the Olympics, the pressure intensifies. My mom and Mrs. Biles had first met back in 2014, and a friendship was growing between our families now that we too lived in the Houston area.

"You need to get her somebody," Mrs. Biles told my mom, "because this is what Simone went through—we know what this looks like. Jordan's been very emotional today. She's been crying. She's had a very tough practice. And I recognize this behavior. Training for the Olympics," she went on, "is a very heavy process. She's gonna need support."

My mom looked over at me and knew that Nellie was right.

When my parents first recommended therapy years before, I immediately shut down at the thought. I went to maybe a handful of sessions, but I resisted the methodology every step of the way, diluting the therapy's effectiveness. Having someone to talk to only really helps when you talk, but my hesitance kept me from pursuing real support. I believed every myth about mental health—I'd bought into the stigma around it.

Something's wrong with you if you need a therapist, and there's nothing wrong with me.

What is my mom doing? There's no way she's going to make me talk to this person for an hour just to, what, go back to what I was doing?

I have been holding and carrying these feelings for so long, how is just talking to a stranger even going to help with that?

This time, my mom and dad talked for weeks about how to bring up the topic of me going to see a therapist without triggering my reflex to avoid it. In the end they took me to dinner and brought up the topic gently. My dad likened therapy to tools in my tool belt that I could pull out when I needed emotional support.

"Nobody says you have to do this forever. And if you don't wanna do it after the first time, you don't have to," he told me. "But at least try to use every tool you have to make you feel successful in every part of your life."

So I decided to really give it a try this time.

When the time came for my first session, I drove there after practice. On the way I was like, *I'm about to turn around. I don't wanna go. What's the point of this?* I was a little early, so I decided to just park in the parking lot to think it through and give my nerves a chance to settle. I was sitting there like, *Okay, Jordan, if you go in here . . . we can go to Dairy Queen.* Yes, I legit bribed myself. It was a treat that I'd rarely been allowed under Coach X's strict dietary restrictions. So, I told myself, "If you go in here, you'll be fine, and then you can treat yourself to some ice cream."

So I got out of the car, and I walked into the therapist's office. I knew that if I canceled or rescheduled, I'd never get started with the process at all.

A receptionist checked me in, and as I sat waiting I had to fight the urge to leave. But I reminded myself that this was a sports psychologist. She had worked with athletes up against some of the same stress to their mind, body, and emotions. Up against the same public expectations and pressures. But I was still worried about whether this white psychologist would be able to relate to me as a young Black woman and the unique stressors and pressures that came with that.

The psychologist finally emerged from her office and ushered me in for our first session. My worries about what I would say flew away almost as soon as I sat down with her. Tears I'd been holding in started to flow. By the end of my first session, I thought to myself, *Man, why am I crying in this place? What is going on? I don't even know this lady and I'm just telling her my whole life story.* The first time I tried therapy, I didn't like having to tell my whole life to a stranger. That just felt so weird. But this time, I pushed through that feeling and kept going. Maybe it was because she made me feel so comfortable. Maybe it was because this time, I was finally just ready.

I told her about how I'd been belittled and made fun of and treated differently than other gymnasts because of the color of my skin. I was able to tell my full truth without having to worry about what others would think of me for finally saying it. At the end of that session, my therapist gave me an assignment: to write down affirmations to myself on sticky notes and put them on my mirror. And I went home and did just that. (Well, after I stopped and got myself that celebratory ice cream.) This practice made me realize that if I could let these things go, then I could bring in more good vibes, good energy, to feel like my normal self again. And it started to work. In the following days, I was able to go into the gym with a different mindset. I was able to actually really think about what I wanted to do with my life with a clearer headspace. I was already feeling lighter.

At each session after that, I was able to open up and tell my therapist even more about my life story. And I broke down into tears almost every time. Because my therapist was also available for virtual sessions, I was able to keep up with my therapy even as my training and travel schedule increased. Working on myself with such focus made me feel more mature and serious. My emotional self deserved the same care I'd devoted to strengthening my body over the years.

We began by identifying and replacing negative thoughts in my head. Each time I thought something bad about myself, I wrote it down and forced myself to think about at least two positive things. Over time, I could see the pattern. I was being so cruel to someone I claimed to love: me.

I remember going through old boxes with my mom around this time and finding photos from the very beginning of my gymnastics career. I looked at them and remembered being told I was too fat even then, when I was such a tiny little girl. Tears streamed down my face as I realized how early the body shaming began and what it took from me.

My therapist put me on the path to rediscovering healthy eating habits and being able to look in the mirror and love what I saw. She noticed that my anxiety and stress went through the roof before big competitions, so we'd schedule more sessions before my meets. Working to figure out what made me feel the best about myself, my sport, and my future made me feel more in control than I'd ever felt—I wasn't just allowing life to *happen*; now I was deciding what was and wasn't best for me, and that felt good. It felt like a new beginning.

*   *   *

At the same time, I was learning that I couldn't expect transformation overnight. My trauma had happened over many years, and my healing would require a similar timetable. There are no mental shortcuts. I had to fully commit to a long journey.

In May, Simone and I were first and second on the leaderboard at the US Classics. I was proud to stand on that podium beside her at the end of the competition. Then at Nationals in June, I placed third behind Simone and Suni Lee. I had made the podium at all three competitions that year, and I was feeling the best I'd ever felt about my chances to finally make the Olympic team. Next up were the Olympic Trials.

*   *   *

The top eight all-around gymnasts from the US Championships automatically qualified for the Trials: Simone, Suni Lee, Emma Malabuyo, Leanne Wong, Jade Carey, Skye Blakely, Grace McCallum, and me. For every Olympics there are new rules that are released, which can include anything from how many people compete on a team to new skill values. For the Tokyo Olympics, there would only be four members of the core team rather than five, plus two event specialists. The change was really geared toward countries that may not be able to qualify an entire team, but had people who are really good in one or two events, like maybe vault or bars, that could potentially make an individual apparatus final. And so, for just that year, they had competitions internationally where you could earn points toward being a specialist for the team. And at the end of that series of competitions, if you were the highest on any of the apparatuses, you earned a berth to the Olympics. Before we even went into the Tokyo Olympic Trials, Jade Carey had clenched her spot as Team USA's specialist.

The Olympic Trials is where you realize that either your career might come to an abrupt end on the other side of this competition, or that it's about to continue to a whole new level. There is no in-between here—the stakes are really *that* high. This *is* the make-it-or-break-it moment that a gymnast trains for their entire life. It all comes down to how well you perform eight routines over two days.

Because the Olympics were delayed this time around, so many athletes didn't even realize they'd now be age eligible to go to the Trials—like Zoe Miller, who was also from

WCC, and Skye Blakely, who had been thirty-five days too young to compete when the Olympics were going to be in 2020, but was eligible in 2021. That additional year also gave athletes time to age into Senior Elite competitions, which had the potential to make the competition for spots on the Olympic team even tighter. But I knew all I could do was focus on what *I* needed to do, with the energy and enthusiasm I'd become known for. I wanted to go out there and just be *myself.*

Because of my performances at the Winter Cup, Classics, and Nationals, many commentators expressed confidence that I would make the Olympic team—the general expectation was that Simone would make the team, hands down, and that Suni and I would vie for the second place spot behind her. Usually just the first person on the leaderboard at the end of Trials is automatically on the US Olympic gymnastics team. For the Tokyo Olympic Trials, the written rule was that it was the first two on the leaderboard. Then the selection committee goes into a room and, within about twenty minutes, they select the rest of the team.

I wanted that second guaranteed spot next to Simone.

But, as an athlete, you have to block out that noise, and that's what I did. A pundit or commentator's positive expectations can put additional pressure on our shoulders or raise our hopes too high, while negative expectations can mire us in self-doubt that can hurt our performances. Expectations, I'd learned time and time again, didn't always add up to the outcome I was looking for. So I knew I had to keep my mind focused. Each and every event, I had no room to waver or fail.

But I struggled in warm-up practices, particularly on the uneven bars. I missed the release from a major transition on high to the Pak salto to the low bar three times during those warm-ups. Over and over as I practiced that move I fell, dropping to the floor when I should have been soaring through the air. I had been solid at my last several competitions, but now the nerves were starting to get to me. I was *so* close to my dream. I could *feel* it. And it was affecting my performance. Because Simone and I were two of the older girls on the team, our coaches took into consideration what our bodies could handle, as well as our mental states, in a different way than they did with the younger girls. Do we need to just chill? Is there something we're struggling with in our lives that means we need extra care? They are always so conscious of each athlete's individual needs.

As Trials started, I reminded myself that I could *not* let my nerves get the best of me. As my dad said to me before every event, "Do your best and forget the rest." *Just land on your feet,* I thought. *Keep your mind clear. You know how to do this.* We're required to salute the judges before and after every routine—that's what we're doing when you see us raising our arms above our heads—and every time I reached for the sky I reminded myself to keep that focus.

On day one, I danced and interacted with the crowd of twenty thousand—the largest crowd I'd ever competed in front of—during the pre-event warm-up, my go-to technique for centering and calming myself. They announced all our names in the arena, and when they got to mine I shot pretend webs from my fingers toward the crowd, a nod to the Spider-Man theme floor music I'd chosen that year. That got laughs, and I was ready to go.

My first event was bars and I hit all of my skills, ending it with a stuck dismount. One down! On beam, I had a mild bobble and then a small adjustment after my leap series, but I stayed on (every gymnast's goal!). I could feel sweat on my face, which showed how nervous I was. That year I learned a new dismount that only a handful of gymnasts can do, as the commentators that night noted. It's called a full-in dismount, and I stuck it cold. I grinned and clapped my hands as I walked off.

I was in fourth place heading into floor. I have a lot of power, so I'm always trying to rein it in. On my first pass, I had a little too much propulsion and landed with one foot out of bounds, but I managed to smile and keep going, and the rest was pretty solid.

Sticking a landing is so difficult, and coming down hard like that is tough on our bodies. In the old days, a step back with one foot was allowed, but that changed in 2008 (it's been speculated that the rise in Achilles injuries might stem from that).

The commentators mentioned how motivated I was to make this team, especially given the 2017 Worlds scenario where I was passed over for the team, in many people's eyes—including mine—unfairly. I'd said in an interview that I just want everyone to see me at 100 percent this time, and it was true. I don't think the public had ever seen that before.

I moved to vault, an easier event for me. I nailed it and ended day one of Trials in third place behind Simone and Suni, a repeat of Nationals just a few weeks prior. But I felt good about that. Suni's score was within striking distance of mine—that second-place spot next to Simone could still be mine. A switch had turned on inside of me over the past several months of those competitions; I felt refocused and ready for this challenge.

I straightened my hair before day two—it's fun just to mix things up—and I wore it in a ponytail with a zigzag part and two braids that night. It made me feel strong and warriorlike. We'd had a day off and I was feeling good.

We started on vault this time. When I'm really on, I can fly on this event, and luckily I did that night. On bars I just floated, as we like to describe it. I could hear the crowd getting behind me, yelling "Come on, Jo!" along with my teammates. There was a huge roar when I stuck that landing as well, and everyone kept loudly rooting for me through beam, which I executed solidly. I practically scampered off the podium at the end. I had just hit the twenty-third of twenty-three straight routines, which is "practically unheard of," as one commentator pointed out, adding, "And you know who she's named after." Michael Jordan's number is twenty-three.

Going into the last rotation of night two at Trials, the floor routine, I was still in third place behind Simone and Suni. I would need a *15.434* on my floor routine in order to get that second locked position. That was a whoppingly high number; the highest score I could possibly get with the level of difficulty my routine entailed was a *15.800*. So I would have to be absolutely perfect to snag second place. But I turned away from the leaderboard and looked at the floor. I could only do what I could. I just wanted to leave it all out there on the floor and see what happened.

As I stood waiting for the cue to begin my routine, I waved my hands at my eyes to dry the tears welling there. This routine was my last chance to show the selection committee what I could do. This was it. This was the last step to making my dream.

I took a deep breath and stepped out onto the floor.

As I went through my routine, the giant screen showing our standings and the playback of my routine as I completed it blurred in the background around me. To focus on that screen for even a second would break my concentration. We never look at that screen. I had to stay present in this moment, in this feeling, in this routine.

Going into my third pass, I was already starting to cry because I knew I was so close. I had to pull myself back—you can't tumble and cry. When I stuck the landing at the end of my last pass the crowd erupted in cheers and roaring applause. I fell to the floor in my final pose of the routine, and then I *really* erupted into tears.

That was it. Now it was in the hands of the judges.

Coach Cécile and Simone greeted me as I stepped off the floor. After a hug from Cécile, Simone wrapped me in a hug too. "I'm so proud of you!" she exclaimed with a squeal. "You did it! That's incredible!" And it was.

I was just a couple of years removed from nearly quitting the sport, thinking it didn't want me anymore, that it had passed me by. But I wasn't done yet. I still had so much more left in me. I saw my score go up, *14.233.* I knew I would be competitive to possibly make a floor final at the Olympics with that type of score. I was thrilled.

* * *

I finished the night in third place behind Simone and Suni. I had consistently ranked top three in all of my competitions that year, and all those gymnastics commentators had been saying they felt confident I'd get a spot . . . As we sat waiting for the selection committee to come back with their answer, I hoped they were right. My teammates and coaches were telling me, "You did an amazing job! Whatever happens, just keep pushing forward and continue your journey." It was an agonizing twenty minutes. I was excited and also crying my eyes out, wondering what was going to happen. So many emotions.

Finally, the moment came. "Please welcome the four members of the 2020 Tokyo Olympic Team!" We were all lined up along the side of the floor, in the shadows so that we couldn't be seen. We'd changed into our red announcement team warm-ups and had each been given a bouquet of red, white, and blue flowers to cradle in one arm as we waved to the crowd. But this year was different than any other year. This year, as we walked out to the applause of the crowd, we all wore COVID masks over our faces.

Shannon Miller, seven-time Olympic medalist and USA Gymnastics Hall of Famer, was announcing the lineup. She said my name third, behind Simone and Suni Lee, and I walked out to join them on the floor with my heart absolutely soaring.

Backstage after the announcement, Simone came up to me and said, "Jordan, I have something for you."

This was surprising. "What do you have?" I asked, and we laughed together. "Wait, was I supposed to get you something?" I was confused—she had been so supportive of me already, she didn't need to give me a present! Then she pulled out a silver necklace with a small pendant of the Olympic rings and handed it to me. "I knew you were going to make this team," she told me. "There was no doubt in my mind."

She explained that she already had the same necklace herself and that she'd gotten one for me and one for Cécile. This would be Cécile's first opportunity to coach at the Olympics (Laurent had coached in 2016 while she supported from the stands), so Simone had bought these necklaces to welcome us both to the Olympics.

"Oh my gosh," I said. I cried a little bit at the sight of it. "Thank you!" I wrapped her in a big hug. "Like, wow, from you, of all people. Thank you. This is crazy!" I couldn't even get my words straight, I was so honored and surprised. "Thank you so much."

13

TOKYO TWISTIES

In less than two years of working with Cécile and Laurent, I had qualified for the 2020 Olympics and was feeling back to myself. After Trials, I signed with GK Elite as my sponsor. I was making a splash in the gymnastics world, and they were now there to whip up any creation I could imagine for my leos. This was possible because of the new Name, Image, and Likeness (NIL) law that had just passed, which allows college athletes to keep their eligibility and make money from sponsorships. Finally, athletes didn't have to choose between going pro and going to college. My teammates and I were among the first gymnasts to benefit from this.

I'd achieved what every gymnast dreams of, but training for the Olympics during the COVID-19 pandemic only heightened the pressure that came with this already difficult feat. Before leaving for the Olympics, we trained nonstop and had to test every day to make sure no one was infected. Because of the pandemic, our families weren't allowed to travel with us to Tokyo. That love and support that sustained me would be absent from my first Olympic Games. Before I flew out for Japan, I made sure to squeeze in several sessions with my therapist so I would be ready mentally as well as physically.

When we eventually arrived in Japan, we had to take a COVID test the minute we stepped off the plane. Tokyo was no joke when it came to testing. That added to our anxiety since we knew that if even one person on our team tested positive, the whole team could be sent home as a safety precaution. If just one of us got COVID, we could cost the entire team its dream.

It was Suni Lee, Grace McCallum, Simone, and me, along with Jade Carey and MyKayla Skinner, the individual event specialists, and the four alternates: Leanne Wong, Emma Malabuyo, Kara Eaker, and Kayla DiCello. We were a team of Olympic newbies, except for Simone, so we all looked to her to lead us. Looking back, I know she felt that pressure from us, added to the pressure the rest of the world was putting on her to repeat her brilliant performance from Rio and come home with gold. *I truly do feel like I have the weight of the world on my shoulders at times*, she wrote on Instagram during that period. *I know I brush it off and make it seem like pressure doesn't affect me but damn sometimes it's hard.* Still, at the time I just thought, *She's Simone. She can do anything.* As she worked to keep team morale high and told us what to expect in the coming days, I hung on every word.

The isolation mixed with a few minor injuries created a

powder keg of pressure on all of us—and the stressors just kept on coming. Before the Olympic Village opened, when we were still staying in a hotel and then being bused to a training center, Kara Eaker tested positive for COVID. I was now very nervous about getting sick myself. The new head of USAG had decided to have us all fly together, train in the same facility, dine together, and ride the bus together (though we sat in staggered rows), so the risks of an infection spreading were very real. We had all come too far to be derailed by this. *I* had come too far.

I called my mom in tears. "They said we can't train because somebody tested positive for COVID." Suni was crying too and Simone was upset. At the time, they still hadn't told us who had tested positive. We all feared that we were going to be sent home, but for now they just put training at a standstill. We had to isolate in our hotel rooms instead. Then word came down that it had been a false positive. They let us train for one session—and then she tested positive again. I called home crying again. I thought all of our dreams were about to end.

I remember waking up alone in my Tokyo hotel room on Monday morning, the day after they isolated us for the second time, thinking, *Well, I could be going home today.* The women's qualifying meet was set to be on Sunday, two days after the opening ceremony for the Games. But we *weren't* sent home; we all remained negative. But Kara and her roommate had to quarantine in their room for the entire ten days.

And we never actually got to stay in the Olympic Village. There, the risk of getting COVID was simply too high, so we were split up into our own individual rooms in a hotel close to the arena, isolated even from one another. Our hotel was basically like a cruise ship—really tiny rooms. We didn't even have outdoor balconies. So several of us moved our tables and chairs from our rooms out to the hallway, setting it up like we were on some patio outside our doors. We would sit at those tables and try our best to have fun together from a distance. We'd color or just chat or try to play cards. We even ate that way. As the self-proclaimed hype woman for our team, I always wanted to make sure everyone was okay, even though me asking them several times a day might have gotten annoying. I didn't care. In between hallway sessions I tried to focus on keeping my mental health steady, drawing and listening to music in my room.

I really had no idea how the isolation might have been impacting the other girls, not even Simone. Bonding as a team was so important to keeping us in a healthy head space, as was the support of our families, who were usually right there building us up and cheering us on. In this strange new world, we didn't have either. All the while our country was expecting us to just do our job, stand strong in the name of bringing medals back home for the US. I don't think anyone could have understood at that time how less than ideal the conditions of our Olympic experience were.

Still, after our COVID spit tests (easier than the nasal swab tests) every morning, we gave it our all in warm-ups and training. The Qualifications competition itself didn't feel like any other I'd been in, not just because these were the Olympics, but because COVID-19 meant there could be no fans in the stands, so the atmosphere was uncomfortably quiet except for light chatter between athletes and coaches. There was no hype from the audience to buoy us. As someone who often enjoyed hyping up the crowd, leading clap-alongs and cheering on my fellow teammates, I felt that missing energy keenly.

That day was so rough for me. I had hit every single routine leading up to the Olympic Trials, but now we were finally here at Qualifications, and it felt like everything just fell apart. At the end of that day, I hadn't qualified for any individual finals, which was something I'd worked toward and felt confident I was capable of. Instead, after team finals I would be watching my teammates from the bleachers. Maybe I didn't belong here after all, I thought.

That night I called home just bawling, begging to get on a plane and fly back to Texas. In that moment, I really meant it. "I failed, I failed," I kept wailing.

"NEVER use those words, Jordan," my mom said. "Now calm down, babygirl. You're at the Olympics because you deserve to be there. You are an Olympian." She used our affirming ritual—making me say my name and repeat that I *was* good enough—but I was crying so hard it was a struggle to get any words out. She reminded me that my team needed me, that no matter how I was feeling I still had a job to do. I calmed down enough for us to pray together. Then I cried myself to sleep.

I woke up in the morning still feeling shaky, but I resolved that I would push through. My team *did* need me. At the end of that day's practice, it was decided I would perform on vault and floor in the team final.

*   *   *

Two days later, the moment had come. Everybody was excited. Team finals: the day we'd all been waiting for.

We were all scuttled into the back gym area of the arena, where teams could warm up and get ready for the meet before it started—but as we were practicing vaults, I noticed Simone getting lost in the air. That's what gymnasts call it when you lose your sense of direction in the middle of a maneuver. Non-gymnasts watching might not notice that anything is wrong at all, but we can tell just by the look of it—maybe they only do one twist when they're supposed to be doing two, or their limbs aren't in the right place as they flip—or even the look on their face when they land. It's a feeling of disorientation, like you've lost control of your body, like your body and mind aren't in sync, and you can't tell up from down. That's a scary feeling, being lost in the air, upside down. In gymnastics we call it "the twisties."

"Are you okay?" I asked Simone. She'd completed the vault but looked dissatisfied with it. Concerned.

As was her way, she brushed it off. "Yeah, I'm good. I'm good."

It's okay, just let her be, I thought. We all had moments of nerves, and even Simone was human. But this was the second time I'd seen her get lost in the air. She'd had another incident the day before at training—she got lost during one of her tumbling passes in her floor routine. But I didn't think much of it at the time. It was strange and uncharacteristic for her, yes, but it happens sometimes with gymnasts. She'd told us she was fighting demons—and we'd all been there. Now, with this second incident, and right before finals, I narrowed my eyes . . . but let it go. I didn't know what to do or what to say to her about it. I wanted to help her, but I also wanted to give her space so she could work through whatever nerves she might be feeling.

She went back to try that vault again, and it was fine. Textbook Simone. I breathed a sigh of relief.

But as we transitioned to the floor to go through our routines one last time before the real deal, she kept telling me, "I don't know where I'm at."

"Okay, just try to get out of your head. You know how to do this. Just do them like you always do," I told her.

I barely warmed up on bars and beam. I was supposed to, but I really just touched the equipment to get used to it. I had my eyes on Simone.

At the end of practice, before the team final was to begin, Simone was like, "Okay, I'm good."

"Okay, cool," I responded. But she didn't look fine to me. As we were heading out onto the competition floor in our red, white, and blue long-sleeved competition leos, you could see on her face that she was not okay. Even later, when I watched footage from the documentary Netflix was making about her, I could see that look on her face—a look of worry and discomfort. Simone is and always has been a woman of facial expressions. When she's upset with how her performances are going, you can see it on her face. Her expression as we were walking out said to me, *I'm concerned. I don't know what I'm going to do, and my mind is not okay.* But she was Simone. I believed she would be fine.

And then, when we started warming up on vault, she did her one touch, warming up on the equipment we would actually be competing on, and got lost. I could see it. Her vault looked funky in the air—not enough rotations. She didn't even land on her feet; she rolled out of that landing, literally doing a somersault on the floor before standing to her feet.

"I'm fine," she said as she came off the mat, before we could even say anything to her. "I'm fine." But now I knew she wasn't fine. I just didn't know what to do about it.

*   *   *

The competition began, and we started on vault. I nailed mine with a near-perfect score. I was still battling nerves, but I had contributed a solid score for Team USA, and getting off to such a great start gave me a boost of confidence. Then it was Simone's turn. I had to turn around, away from the vault. I couldn't bear to look, and I had this sinking feeling in my gut. I thought, *I do not know what this girl is going to do. I just need her to land on her feet. I don't need her getting injured, none of that.* But I also realized I couldn't leave her hanging like that. If something was wrong, I needed to be there to see it through with her. I turned back around, and we locked eyes in that mostly empty arena.

"You're good, bro," I reassured her. "You are good. You're solid."

She nodded to herself. Then saluted. And as she ran down that vault runway, she blocked in her mind. And she got lost in the air.

Since she's so powerful, she went really high, so a non-gymnast might have thought she looked fine. But we all knew she wasn't. Anyone else would have broken their neck and not been able to land what she did on that vault.

The entire team was watching, tense with nerves, leaning forward in anticipation with gritted teeth and clenched fists.

Luckily, she landed on her feet. But I had no words because I could see in her eyes that she was just devastated.

What do we do what do we do what do we do? What's she going to do? I kept saying in my head as she stepped off the mat. "I'm fine," she spat out.

No, she definitely wasn't fine.

As I stood there listening, Simone said to our coaches, "I don't know what I'm going to do the rest of the meet. That's my problem. I just don't want to do anything stupid."

Simone walked out of the arena to talk to our doctors to figure out what she was going to do. Coach Cécile followed her out of the arena. When Cécile came back, a few minutes later, she walked straight over to me and said, "Jordan, put your grips on."

"Huh?" I looked at her, flabbergasted. "I'm not doing bars. What do you mean?" I was only supposed to compete in two events: vault and floor, which would be our final event. To put my grips on meant that *I* was going to be competing in bars. Not Simone. But where *was* Simone? What did that mean? I was so confused.

"Put your grips on," she repeated. "You're going on bars for Simone."

In the years since the Rio Olympics, Simone had trained to come back and do it all again but even better—not something many gymnasts are able to do. There's no way she would make the decision to pull out unless she was having serious problems. I was glad she knew her body well enough not to perform any risky skills that could prove fatal if she was even a fraction of an inch off. I was in shock and my eyes filled with tears. *Put your grips on* . . . I was so upset for Simone, but I wiped away the tears. I knew how much these Olympics meant to her and the road we'd been on together to get here. If she needed me to fill in for her, then that's what I'd do.

Simone came back into the arena, over to us, and brought us all into a huddle. We all stared at her, wide-eyed, as she spoke to us calmly.

"Okay, guys, I need you to continue this competition without me." Suni and I looked at each other and started tearing up immediately. What did she mean? What was she talking about?

Bro, ain't no way! I thought to myself. *This is* crazy!

"You guys *got* this," she said. This was the moment that we all saw a different Simone. She was firm and so, *so* serious. She looked us in the eyes and we all listened. "You *got* this."

She hugged me, then Suni. "I love you guys, and you're going to be just fine. You guys have trained for this." She could see how concerned we were for her. Photographers stood in a line just feet away from us as she reassured us, "I'll be fine," then pulled her white sweatpants over her competition leo. With Simone unable to continue, it meant that Team USA would be competing with only three gymnasts, compared to the other countries, who had four.

Everything was a haze. I don't even remember doing it, but I know that I competed in bars for Team USA that day. The girl who'd had so little confidence in herself when she first came to WCC was now being asked to stand in for the greatest gymnast of all time. That was crazy for me to even think about. But in that moment I was just like, *Okay, I'm gonna be doing this for her, myself, everyone around us, because these scores need to count in order for us to get a medal.*

In my head, I kept repeating that scripture my mom had suggested I use as a mantra—Philippians 4:13, "I can do all things through Christ who strengthens me." Even if and when I fall short, there is that scripture buoying me. And this time would be the same. We were a team, representing our country, and I needed to do this for the millions of supporters we had watching us and rooting for us back home who wanted to see Team USA on the podium.

When I tell you that everything from that moment onward that day was a complete blur, I mean it. Everything seemed to be moving so fast, swirling around me, while I was still in my head, wondering and worried about my friend. I couldn't turn that part of my mind off. But at the same time . . .

Oh my gosh, I'm doing bars. Like—what? There's no way.

We were in second place behind the Russian team going into the bars rotation. I was determined to hit the routine and I did—it was solid. Afterward I threw my arms up in the air and I screamed, *Let's go!* to a near empty arena but I didn't care. It was about the team. Grace, Suni, and I all aced beam, with Simone screaming from the sidelines like a proud mother.

I would love to end this story saying that I was perfect that day, but I wasn't. I went in to my floor routine feeling

confident but on my third floor pass, which had been giving me trouble, I sat it down. But Suni, who was the one
to fill Simone's shoes on floor, put together a beautiful
routine. We were all so proud of ourselves in that moment.
We had given it all we had, and that day we didn't lose the
gold medal, we won the silver.

14

I'M NOT DONE YET

They called us the "Fighting Four." Simone, Grace, Suni, and me. It was such a fitting name, reflecting the difficulty we'd experienced. We had won silver against all odds, with only three of us competing and despite all the pressure we were under.

It's monumental to walk away from the Olympics with even a memory, let alone a silver medal. But my initial reaction to our silver medal was disappointment. *If Simone were out there*, I thought, *we would've had gold.*

At the end of the competition, when we were about to get our medals, I started crying.

"Why are you crying?" Simone asked me. "You're an Olympic medalist. Why are you crying?"

"I feel like I disappointed you," I said, wiping away tears.

"Disappointed?" I could tell she was a little confused and incredulous.

"Yes. I feel like I disappointed you. Because you—we—wanted gold so bad, and I feel like it was my fault."

She was like, "Jordan, look at me." I did, raising my eyes to meet hers with some difficulty. "It's *no one's* fault. It's not my fault; it's not your fault. It's no one's fault. You didn't just *get* a silver medal. You *won* that silver medal. You *earned* that silver medal. You literally helped the team get that silver medal. You made me so proud."

I nodded to myself, taking those words in. "You know what? You're right." I laughed a bit. "Like, that's so crazy just to think about."

When they handed me my silver on the podium, I was smiling behind my mask. Then I looked at Simone and told her, "Next time it'll be gold."

*   *   *

Ever since that moment, when people have asked me, "So how do you feel about getting silver?" I respond with "I didn't just *get* that. I *won* that." Remembering what we all went through—the stress, the expectations, the isolation—makes me appreciate that medal all the more.

When we got off the plane back home in Houston, there were crowds of people standing right at the gate waiting for us, holding signs and cheering. I hadn't expected such a big, warm reception and was taken completely, pleasantly off guard. *Is all of this for us?* I wondered as Simone and I, with Laurent and Cécile, stepped into the cheering swarm. Photographers flashed their cameras, and our families wrapped us in long-awaited hugs. They hadn't been able to be there for us in Tokyo, but they could be there for us now.

There were signs reading *I LOVE Biles & Chiles!* Children were there in T-shirts with our names on them. That is a moment I'll never forget. We had inspired whole families to leave their homes and wait for our flight to land—and in that moment I realized that we'd probably even inspired a next generation of gymnasts. That was such a special feeling. I wish I'd had more gymnasts who looked like us to look up to when I was their age.

After we left the airport there was a parade for us. I was sticking my head out of a car's sunroof, waving at all these people chanting our names. It was outstanding. But the best part of the day was being able to celebrate with our families afterward. My family and I went to a restaurant called Uncle Julio's. Over enchiladas and chips and guac, I told them my stories about Tokyo. Back at the house, Grandpa Gene had decorated my bedroom door with balloons. I took my medal out of its case and put it around his neck. I was finally home.

*   *   *

I got two more tattoos after the Tokyo Olympics: the Olympic rings, which were such an honor to have inscribed on my skin, and then while we were on the "Gold Over America Tour" in the fall I got the word *Golden*, which was our motto, symbolizing the gold that was inside each of us.

After Tokyo, I was hesitant to talk about stepping in for Simone at first. Everyone online wanted to know the intimate details of what we'd been through, and that felt so invasive. We'd already given so much, and it just felt like everyone demanded more, more, *more* at every turn. But I realized that this was partly my story, and I should be the one telling it.

So in late 2021, a few months after returning from Tokyo, I joined Taraji P. Henson for an interview on her digital series *Peace of Mind*. She's not only an actress but also a mental health advocate, and I opened up to her about the pressures and experiences that we elite athletes face, particularly under the tutelage of abusive coaches. That interview with her was the first time I'd ever publicly spoken about my experiences with Coach X and how I'd had to fight my way back to happiness. I was proud to be part of the movement that was starting, transforming the way we think about mental health, especially for elite athletes.

After opening up about my experiences, I was met with overwhelming love and support from other athletes, fans, and journalists. I felt confident knowing that the generation coming behind me would experience more support than we had, and that, because people like me were speaking up, things would change for the better. It was still scary to think about those who would downplay my pain because of the success they saw. As I told Taraji in that conversation, when people question how I could be unhappy while winning medals, or discredit the need for mental health breaks in athletics, I've learned to seek validation from within rather than their exterior approval.

I'd learned a really valuable lesson that pulled me from the dark place I thought I'd never claw my way out of: things *can* change for the better. Just three years since I'd thought about quitting, I had transformed my relationship to gymnastics, my body, my coaches, and all of the global attention I was garnering. I was and still am grateful to

Simone for helping me put my mental health first, but I also know that it shouldn't be on the gymnasts to figure out how to *survive* the sport. Elite gymnastics must improve as a sport so that girls like me aren't trading our mental health for a medal. The demands for perfection, with so little institutional support, lead to mental health crises, which could be prevented with new coaching standards, a cultural shift around what a gymnast's body should look like, and more mental health services for athletes. Luckily, thanks in part to gymnasts like Simone and me speaking out, the sport is starting to take mental well-being as seriously as physical fitness.

* * *

After deferring my initial acceptance at UCLA, I finally started class in January 2022, when I was twenty years old. That's also when I got my first dog, Chanel, a chocolate-colored toy poodle. It helped to have an emotional support pup with me, my little cuddle bug. I started out majoring in business economics, but I eventually switched to sociology. After all I'd been through, I think I wanted to understand more about people.

With one Olympics under my belt, I was ready to get back to the books while also competing on the UCLA gymnastics team. I'd chosen UCLA, way back when I was a seventh grader, because it's a vibe: the California sunshine and proximity to Los Angeles—not to mention that UCLA was close to major zoos and my lifelong addiction, Jamba Juice, was on campus. But my parents also made me consider the strong academics that UCLA offered, and they were right about that too. Over the years, my family and I had gone to watch the UCLA Bruins gymnastics team compete against the University of Washington, not too far from where we lived, cheering in the stands as I got used to the idea that one day this would be my school. Now that moment was finally here.

Being a college student gave me more freedom than I'd ever had before. I made friends and actually had time to hang out with them! More than that, NCAA gymnastics allows for a lot more personality in our performances, and there were so many meets that I got more comfortable with them than ever before. Using hip-hop or R & B music in my routines would have been frowned upon in elite gymnastics, but I decided to really put my own self on the floor in the NCAA. I went viral with my first NCAA floor routine my freshman year, performed to a medley of Normani and Lizzo. We even threw in some hip-hop dance. I was proud of myself for pushing the envelope and breaking the mold. The older NCAA judges frowned upon it, but when the video of that performance went viral, I saw that it might be accepted in the culture, if not in collegiate and elite gymnastics, and that was enough for me right then.

Collegiate scoring is so different from elite international scoring. You aren't rated on separate difficulty and execution scores in NCAA gymnastics, and the level of difficulty required there is lower. Also you can actually get a perfect ten, which is impossible in modern elite gymnastics.

I was excited to be on campus, and I wanted to be content with where I'd landed. But life as a Bruin brought its own challenges, reminding me that what I'd faced as a Black woman in gymnastics wasn't exclusive to the elite level. Not long before I arrived on campus, a white teammate had said the n-word while singing a song at practice. Though I wasn't there when it happened, my phone immediately blew up with calls and texts from my new UCLA teammates venting their outrage. This wasn't quite the welcome to the team I'd been hoping for all those years leading up to finally coming to campus.

Coming less than a year after the murder of George Floyd and the global racial justice protests that followed, that racist act called out for a strong response. But our coaching staff was slow to act and actually urged those of us who were hurt and offended to be more open to the white teammate's perspective. Be more open to *their* perspective? As national media picked up on the entire controversy, the team was warned that *we* might jeopardize the white student's mental health. *What about the Black students' mental health?* No mention was made of our well-being at all. I'd seen this play out before, where people of color who'd been hurt were asked to center someone else's feelings—their *aggressors'* feelings. The whole situation drained and triggered me.

There was another reason I wasn't feeling entirely comfortable at UCLA—the school had started getting letters addressed to me from stalkers who had seen me on TV, and campus security and local police were on alert. *Maybe,* I thought to myself, *this isn't where I want to be right now.*

With the Olympics already a goal achieved, I could have decided I'd hit my peak, but it kept gnawing at me that I'd never made a World Championships team. I had attempted it many times over the years, but Coach X's belligerent style of training me—and then my own lack of preparation as I considered leaving the sport altogether—had gotten in the way on a few separate occasions. Now that I was feeling more confident in my skills and wanted a break from the chaos on campus, I decided it was time to address this unfinished business. After Worlds, I would make my final decision on whether being a Bruin was truly for me.

*   *   *

Coming out of my freshman year, I set my focus on going to the 2022 US Gymnastics Championships to try to make the US team for Worlds. This was when I started my now-annual ritual of setting myself a theme for every elite season to keep focused and motivated through whatever hardships life dealt out. My theme for 2022 was *Little Miss Not Done Yet*. I had more to give—both to myself and to my sport.

As I stepped into my mint green leotard and began to do my hair and makeup for the US Gymnastics Championships in August, I chose to keep my look simple, pulling my hair into a high bun with a bow. That day I just wanted to focus on one event at a time, and let everything else blur around me. I wouldn't even pay attention to my scores or anyone else's.

On day two of the championships, I came back to do it all again—now in a fuchsia-and-black leotard, a nod to one of Lupita Nyong'o's red carpet looks. Again, I focused only on having consistent performances across each event. Halfway through that competition night, I felt pretty good about my chances of placing. Later, my coach came up to me and whispered that I was likely going to place third in the all-around. That brought a smile to my face even before I realized that the two girls ahead of me were also Black. And after I landed my dismount on bars, I knew for sure we were good. I saw my name go up in that third spot and I thought, *Wow, we just did something—three Black girls.* Somewhere in the bleachers, my dad later told me, he turned to my mother and mouthed, *All-Black podium.* My mom nodded back at him, understanding how monumental this would be for Black gymnasts everywhere.

At the start of the medals ceremony, I stepped onto the third-place rostrum cradling my bouquet and finally realizing the honor and gravity of what was about to happen.

I watched as Shilese Jones and then Konnor McClain assumed their positions on the second- and first-place rostrums respectively. By the time we stepped off that podium we were already going viral on social media. For the first time in gymnastics history, Black women gymnasts filled all three podium spots.

Afterward, some of white America started grumbling online. "Why does this have to be considered a *Black* moment? Why do you make everything about race? Can't we all just be American?" These kinds of comments showed a clear lack of understanding that this was truly a groundbreaking moment for American gymnastics. The sport has historically struggled to have more than one Black star at once. Dianne Durham, the first Black woman to win the all-around senior title at the women's US National Championships back in 1983. Then "Awesome Dawesome," Dominique Dawes, who broke several records including being a three-time Olympian; then Gabby Douglas, who picked up where Dianne Durham left off and became the first Black woman to win the all-around title at an Olympic Games. And then, of course, the GOAT, Simone Biles, who has more all-around titles than any gymnast of any gender, nationality, or race. Each of these women changed the game and opened the door for more Black girls behind them. Now *we* were changing the game, despite the systemic issues we'd faced across our years in the sport. We were letting it be known that Black gymnasts—who'd been chided both within the sport and online for everything from our hair to our physical statures and critiqued as not being as "graceful" as white gymnasts—were here to stay. Finally, we saw Black women winning across the board.

Understanding that I'd just accomplished something that would likely be in the history books was the most surreal feeling I'd ever had. I'd been training for nearly my entire life with the goal of winning medals, but I now understood how much my presence in the sport actually meant—to other Black and Latino people, to the gymnasts who would come after me who looked like me. A year after we were the first all-Black gymnastics podium, Simone Biles and Shilese Jones of the USA and Rebeca Andrade of Brazil took the podium at Worlds in Antwerp—the first *international* all-Black podium. The glass ceiling was finally shattered, ensuring that even more of us could take up space without needing to take turns.

With that 2022 competition, I also became one of the first gymnasts (alongside my Team USA teammate Jade Carey) to compete at the elite level while remaining an NCAA gymnast. This was unprecedented. That's partly because of the myth that women gymnasts are at their best around the young age of sixteen or so, which means many of them don't stay in elite gymnastics long enough to be college gymnasts at the same time. For women, college gymnastics often signals retirement from the elite level of competition.

Later that year, I made the Worlds Team for the first time in my career and traveled to Liverpool with the rest of Team USA. I'd *finally* achieved this lifelong goal. I won team gold and individual silver medals for my vault and floor performances. I'd achieved what I'd set out to do, and it was time to decide whether to return to collegiate gymnastics or not. (I hadn't left school entirely—I was taking my fall classes online.) Since I'd been gone, our Bruins coach had been replaced. The new head coach gave me confidence that Black student athletes would be respected and valued as human beings the same way our white peers were. So, I prepared to head to Los Angeles and rejoin my teammates for the term beginning in January.

Under our new coaches, UCLA performed better than ever in competitions that year. I was working with the team's choreographer to include my own culture and '90s hip-hop music in my NCAA floor routine and wanted to continue using it all the way into the elite season. But Donatella Sacchi, president of the FIG's Women's Artistic Gymnastics Technical Committee, told my coaches that my music might not be received well by the international gymnastics community. I took this as code for my music was too "cultural" for them. So I ultimately decided against it and created another routine for elite competitions.

I set national individual records with the top all-around score in the entire country that season—and held national titles on both floor and bars, helping UCLA get back to the NCAA Championships. I was thrilled and felt like I was finally stepping into my own, fully. Going to therapy hadn't miraculously solved all of my problems, but it helped me to better navigate life's challenges.

But there was a personal tragedy that made that spring incredibly tough for me. In March, just before the NCAA regional championships, my Auntie Crystal died. She had lung cancer and had been living with my parents for a few months after her diagnosis. I'd flown home to see her when she was hospitalized toward the end, and she wanted me and only me in the room with her one night.

In our family we're people of faith—God is our number one, and we definitely believe in angels. That night, Auntie Crystal drifted in and out of consciousness, at one point trying to pull all the intravenous tubes out of her arms. "You can't go home, Auntie," I told her. "You need to stay here." She kept shaking her head and pointing to the security camera in the corner of the room. I couldn't figure it out, but finally I said, "You mean you're ready to go home, as in HOME?" And she nodded her head yes. I honestly think she could have been seeing an angel when she kept pointing at the camera.

I didn't tell anyone else in the family, because everyone still wanted to have hope, but she died just a day later. Auntie Crystal was telling me without telling me that it was her time to go.

The grief was crushing. I had never lost anyone so close to me. As the flood of emotions kept coming, I had to tell myself what I said back in 2018: *I'm not okay.* The difference between 2023 and 2018 was that now, I had the tools to take care of myself and turn to people I loved rather than isolating myself and succumbing to depression.

I turned to the routine comforts in my life, like binge-watching Netflix, napping, scrolling through Pinterest, eating with friends, or just having space to myself, to focus on my own needs. I also got my second dog, Versace, aka Ace, another toy poodle. These methods of self-care helped me refind joy.

I got through the NCAA National Championships in April, even as I was grieving. We didn't make it to the finals, but I was proud of how our team performed. Individually I won both the bars and floor national titles. But I was physically and mentally exhausted. I took some time off from training and when I returned, I decided 2023's theme should be *Run It Back* since my 2022 season had been so successful. Because I'd taken a training break, I wasn't as prepared heading into the US Classics or the US Championships in August. Reminding myself that Auntie Crystal would want me to keep fighting and competing emboldened me as I headed to Santiago, Chile, for the Pan American Games.

Though this was my first time at Pan Ams, I was the veteran elite gymnast of our team. Now it was my turn to help support the younger gymnasts, as older gymnasts had once supported me, helping to set the tone of morale while maintaining the standard of discipline we needed to reach the podium. I also got to be the team flag bearer, a dream I'd held since watching the Rio Olympics. But it turned out to be a bittersweet moment because a passport issue kept my mom and dad from being able to attend. They had been present at almost all of my competitions, so I felt their absence in Chile keenly. But I knew they had tried everything they could to be there. Now it was up to me to trust that I had what I needed inside of me to emerge a winner.

In the end, we won team gold and I took home a silver on vault and a bronze in the all-around.

*   *   *

And then came another blow, and this one nearly flattened me. Grandpa Gene passed away on the day before Thanksgiving. I couldn't believe he was gone. The good memories all flooded back. Like the time he refused, as usual, to supposedly jinx me by coming to one of my meets—and then we got home after I'd placed first to find he'd bought a Mylar balloon that said "#1" and fastened it to a barbell on our front lawn. He wanted the entire neighborhood to know his granddaughter had won. Or how he taught me all about cars and would always call to ask if I'd changed the oil (I'm a girl who doesn't like to get dirty, so nope). I got a tattoo on my forearm of what he would say to us all the time: *Where you are, I have been. Where I am, you will be.* Like the cross on my wrist, this tattoo reminds me my grandpa is always with me, no matter what. I wouldn't be where I am right now if it weren't for him.

I was in deep emotional and physical anguish trying to process these huge losses in my life. *Run It Back?* The year 2023 was not paying any attention to the theme I'd chosen.

But the devastation of losing my grandpa also helped clarify something in my mind: I was definitely going to pursue my Olympic dream for 2024. My mom says she and my dad could tell I was *saying* I would go for it earlier in 2023, but in my heart and mind I hadn't fully made the decision. My grandpa always told me, "You're going to make it to Paris," and my auntie had also been very much in support. They believed I had it in me to try again. Finally, my heart was in it too.

15

BUDDY SYSTEM

I n late 2023, I went to my first Beyoncé concert, and it inspired my theme for 2024. Because Destiny's Child was already huge when I was born, I've never known a world without Beyoncé, so I thought to myself, *I'mma go to this Beyoncé concert, and just see who she is in person.* I also watched her documentary and was so inspired that she, as a childhood star, had gone through so many hardships but still came out on top. Her song "I'm That Girl" became my theme song and motto for 2024. The phrase was not meant as a cocky thing, but as a reminder that I'm finally confident enough in myself and my skills to proudly proclaim in the bathroom mirror, *I'm that girl.*

It turned out I would need that theme to help get me through the challenges about to come my way. In February, right before our National Team camp, I sprained the AC joint in my right shoulder while training. When I landed hard on that shoulder and felt searing pain, I was sure I'd fractured it, but with the grace of God, the MRIs and X-rays that my coaches sent me to get showed it was only a sprain. Still, I was in pain 24/7 and couldn't do anything for a solid two to three weeks. I could lift my shoulder, but I couldn't bear weight at all. I had to withdraw from the Winter Cup. I didn't want to start sowing doubt about my prospects in the runup to the Olympic Trials. So the media was told I couldn't compete because I wasn't feeling well—and I did have a sinus cold. But that injury was really the clincher.

Yet the US Classics was coming up in May, and I thought to myself, *I can't take any more time off.* So I pushed myself harder to recover—I needed to be at my very best to be a contender for the upcoming Olympics. Then, in March, I injured my knee on a tumbling pass. An ultrasound showed I had a deep bone bruise, and it proved to be absolutely debilitating. I could feel my 2024 Olympic dreams slipping between my fingers. Every day I was taping, icing, doing physical therapy, trying to figure out if my knee was ever going to go back to normal.

Finally, when it wasn't getting better, a team camp doctor sent me for an MRI—and in April I learned that I had actually fractured my fibula and torn my LCL doing that tumbling pass, but both were on their way to healing.

I kept these injuries out of the media too—no negativity wanted or needed. I was medically cleared for training just three weeks before Classics, where I ended up somehow taking third place all around. It was crazy! I did okay in the US Championships later that month too—I placed fifth. Olympic Trials, come and get me.

*   *   *

The US Olympic Trials is the biggest meet you'll ever do in your life, as I always say. I've always felt that it's the hardest one of the four competitions leading up to the Olympics, even harder than the Olympics itself. *Making* the Olympics is more mentally grueling than actually *being* at the Olympics because, historically, the United States has been dominant in the sport of gymnastics. We've had the best girls, especially over these last several quads (the four-year stretches in between Olympics). So, at the Trials, you're truly going against the very best of the best. The competition was the fiercest I would be up against, and making it here meant that I could make it anywhere.

But I remembered my coaches' voices in my head: *Remember, you can't control the uncontrollables. You can only control what* you *do, not what happens after that. Pay attention to yourself,* they told me. *Make sure you're in your own bubble.* That always reminds me to keep my head in the game and just focus on what *I'm* supposed to be doing.

We left for Olympic Trials on June 22, flying to Minneapolis days ahead of the first day of the competition, which would start on the twenty-seventh. The flight from Texas took the better part of the day, so we didn't have practice when we got there. We went to the hotel, and Simone and I shared a room.

We fell asleep early and woke up the next morning to what we call accommodation day. It's the day we spend just getting used to the time zone change (if we've come from far away) and to the equipment that we'll be on. There are three major brands of gymnastics equipment that most elite gymnasts use. We take the time to test and get accustomed to the apparatus before each competition because there can be subtle variations among them (the bounciness of the uneven bars, for instance). These slight differences can affect your performance, if you're not prepared for them. But because I got to the elite level at such a young age, I've encountered all the brands, and the differences don't faze me much anymore.

When I woke up that morning, I lay in bed staring up at the ceiling. I couldn't believe I had made it to Trials again. The moment felt utterly surreal. I pulled myself out of bed: Simone was now up and moving about the room too. In the bathroom I looked at myself in the mirror. *This doesn't seem real. How am I here again?* I thought to myself, locking eyes with the Jordan in the mirror. I took a second to close my eyes and let that sensation of wonder and appreciation wash over me. *I am so proud of you,* I told myself. I repeated this over and over again in my head.

For me, at this point, it was about beating myself more than it was about beating other people. I wanted to do better than I had in Tokyo—better than *I* had ever done. I looked in that mirror and was no longer the young girl who wanted to beat everybody else. I now just wanted to beat *myself,* so I'd know, at the end of it, whatever that outcome is, *I've done what I need to do.*

I took a deep breath and stepped away from the mirror. Time for go mode. Time to switch on. I grabbed my makeup bag and looked at Simone. "Yo, we're here again! Like, this is crazy!" I laughed.

We put on our makeup. I checked my watch and saw that it was almost time to head out to the team bus that would shuttle us to the Target Center Arena for our ten-o'clock practice. When we're in that competition setting, *everything* is timed and scheduled: when we have to get on the bus, when we can eat. At the same time that *we're* competing and being selected for the Olympics, the men gymnasts are doing the same, so we have to go back and forth between when they have the arena and when we do. They were to compete Thursday and Saturday; we competed Friday and Sunday.

After stretching, we hit the equipment wearing our short-sleeved training leos. Training leos are short-sleeved because they're more comfortable, and competition leos are always long-sleeved, offering more decoration and glam for our performances. It was a light day at practice because we knew that the days ahead of us would be so intense.

Podium Training is the most hardcore day of all. At Podium Training, which was the Wednesday before the competition was to begin on Friday, you do everything full-out. Full vaults, full floor routine, full bar routine, full beam routine. It's your time to get used to what it's going to be like at the meet—but it's also where the scrutiny on us increases. The eyes on us are silently assessing, judging: *Who's prepared? Who's ready? Who can last and stay strong and continue performing their best for a whole month of Olympic pressure?* At Podium, we even have to "salute" our routines to our coaches and our head selection committee. We saluted our routines as if we were really at the meet, and then we received mock scores from the judges. They would let us know, "This would count toward your score; this wouldn't count toward your score," or they would advise us of what we should keep or consider taking out of our routines.

They're starting to consider who looks ready, even before the Trials competition begins.

Three girls fell to injuries at Trials, one of them before the end of Podium Training. The Olympic Trials hadn't even formally begun yet, and Skye Blakely's dream of making the 2024 Olympics was already over.

Skye got injured doing one of her tumbling passes, a double layout full-out. I saw the moment she hit the floor and didn't get back up. She yelped, unable to pull herself to her feet, tears streaming down her face.

From the way she hobbled when the coaches helped her out of the arena, I had a feeling it was an Achilles tear. I'd been around this sport for so long, I could spot one when I saw it. Even my own Achilles tendons were weak after years of gymnastics, and I winced too, watching her getting hauled out. *That could happen to me*, I thought.

At the Tokyo Trials, Skye had injured herself moments before the competition started, as she was practicing her vault, and had to pull out. Now, again, she was injured at Trials, right before competing for her lifelong dream. Moments like that are so hard to watch. Every injury means a dream ruined or a career possibly ending. And when an athlete gets injured like that, they get whisked away, out of the arena, and we don't know where they go exactly. Are they just in the locker room? Was it really bad and they're en route to the hospital? We can text them our well-wishes and condolences, but for a while, it's like they just vanish. Skye's injury intensified the grueling anxiety we were all under. Those things could happen to any of us.

But I heard Cécile and Laurent in my head after so many

years of repetition. *Pay attention to yourself. Make sure you're in your own bubble.*

I reminded myself of these words and turned back to what I was doing.

* * *

Back at the hotel after Podium, I got straight into the shower to wash away the chalk. I don't like when chalk is on me. It leaves me with this disgusting feeling like I'm covered in dirt, so I always shower as soon as I get home.

For Simone and me, rooming together is always so chill. I might get out of the shower to find her FaceTiming with her husband, Jonathan, or we might just say, "Yo, what are we eating? You want some sushi?" That night we ordered spicy tuna rolls and a California roll from Uber Eats.

Once I'm out of the arena or out of practice, I don't think about gymnastics. I think about *What am I going to do with my family? What am I going to eat? Am I going to go shopping? Do I need my nails done?* I can't keep gymnastics and my life in the same headspace, or I start overthinking everything. Here at Trials, I was still keeping the torn LCL and fractured fibula I'd suffered back in March on the DL. I didn't want to use it as an excuse or have the media's view of my performance colored by it. I was fully healed, but the injuries had really cut into my training time, so I worried about the effects of that. Luckily therapy helped me to reinforce that healthy boundary in my mind, to compartmentalize. *Gymnastics is what you do, not who you are.* So, in those moments of quiet, when I was making sure worries about the

Trials didn't creep into my mind, my thoughts would go to my auntie Crystal and grandpa Gene, and the unshakable faith they both had in me. They'd believed I could do it, so I *would* do it.

The morning after Podium was Thursday. It was the men's first day of competition, which meant we had only the morning to practice since the men would be taking up the arena in the afternoon. That morning I practiced bars and beam.

Afterward I went back to the locker room area to cold-tub my ankles with Simone, Joscelyn Roberson, Dulcy Caylor, and Tiana Sumanasekera. Cold-tubbing helps with reducing inflammation in ankle sprains or strains. Josc, Dulcy, and Tiana were both from the World Champion Centre with Simone and me and we trained together. As we sat chatting at the edge of the tub, our feet icy numb, Simone asked, "Wanna get in the hot tub with me?"

"Sure, let's do it." We pulled our feet from the water and waved goodbye to Josc, Tiana, and Dulcy. In our bikinis, Simone and I got into the hot tub.

"It's starting today." I grinned as we slipped into the water. "I hope the men do good!"

"They will! We're rooting for them. I'm just trying to get back to this hotel to take a nap!" She laughed. "I'm gonna need it!"

"Me too." I sighed.

We sat in the hot tub, our hair up in buns, and played around on TikTok. Simone posted a video of us dancing in the water with Jordan Adetunji's "Kehlani" playing. It was our moment to just be silly and let loose, letting all the other noise from our lives and our practices, from the hopes and mounting pressures on our shoulders, slip away. Simone captioned the TikTok video, *ready for day 1 tomorrow! part of our olympic trials recovery.* It was mental recovery at its very best, just letting loose and leaving all the pressures momentarily behind.

16

I'M THAT GIRL

F riday morning, I woke up to Qualifications day with a fire burning in my core that said I wanted it bad. Another shot at making the Olympic team! I knew I had to go out there and give it absolutely everything I had.

"We're competing today!" I exclaimed, to help psych Simone and me up.

"Yup, we're competing today." She laughed.

I'd catch myself saying this, practically chanting it, all day. Both to myself and out loud to the other girls. "We're competing today! We're competing today!" I was right at the doorstep of my dream, and I needed to get hyped about it. We went easy in that morning's practice. No way we were going to push too hard and risk injury just hours before competing. I practiced beam and bars again. Skye came down to our practice on crutches. I looked across the arena at her for a long moment as she got settled on a bench. It was so hard to see her like that, to know that she had been on her feet just a day or so before and now would not be competing with us at all. Emotions were running high, but she still wanted to come support us.

"Good luck! And have *fun*!" she cheered us on. The rest of us said this to one another throughout practice. *Good luck. Have fun. We're competing today!*

Back on the bus, we headed to the hotel to put on our competition leos and to do our hair and makeup, but the ride was tense and quiet. We all huddled in our own corners of the bus, earbuds in, as was typical on a competition day. We were hours away from the bright lights, from the adoring eyes of the audience and assessing stares of the judges. Everybody was trying to mentally prepare for what we were about to do, for what was on the line.

At the hotel, Simone ordered us sandwiches from Firehouse Subs. We ate quickly, then lay down to take quick naps. The moment we woke up, Simone turned on her playlist and music filled the room. We vibed out to Chris Brown, Beyoncé, and Megan Thee Stallion, as I stood in the bathroom mirror putting on my foundation and trying to figure out what kind of cut crease I wanted in my eyeshadow. I was in my zone, and she was in hers. In that flow state, we don't need many words. We move around each other with a comfortable fluidity as we do our makeup. When it's time to do our hair, she'll either ask me for one braid or two, depending on how she's feeling. I sat Simone down in the hotel chair and stood behind her to do her single braid leading up to her high bun for day one of Trials. I pulled my hair back into a tight, sleek bun and topped it off with a red, white, and blue bow to match our day one competition leos. That first day of competition, our leotards had red bottoms with a blue-and-white-crystal-encrusted torso. I called my parents to pray like I usually do before competitions. By this time, it was three or four o'clock in the afternoon. Time to head to the arena to meet our destinies.

By the time seven o'clock rolled around, and the arena filled with the roar of the audience, we were ready for showtime.

*   *   *

Cheers erupted in my ears. The screams were deafening, rippling throughout the crowd, shaking the rafters of Target Center Arena. We gymnasts were lined up in our white tracksuits behind the partition separating us from the open floor of the arena and the audience, waiting to run out for our introduction. I closed my eyes and prayed as the vibrations of the cheers thrummed through the floor and up into my feet.

God, please watch over me. Have your angels watch over me so nothing happens. Please help me have the best meet of my life.

Then the familiar countdown began, as the emcee got the crowd hyped for day one of the competition.

Ten.

Nine.

Eight!

The giant screen overhead filled with the video compilation of our individual highlights. Each girl would run out to greet the crowd during her own short highlight video, her name in lights around the arena. From where we were lined up we couldn't see the video, but we all grinned to ourselves as we heard the love from the audience. We knew that our names were flashing larger than life across the screen and around the room, and the love of the fans wrapped us in its embrace. We ran out one by one as the emcee called our names, raising both hands high as we waved to the crowd. My 2022 Worlds teammate Shilese Jones had injured her knee during vault warm-ups, so she ran out with her leg taped up underneath her tracksuit. By the time Simone was called, you couldn't even hear the emcee say her name, the roars of applause for her were so deafening. I was excited for her and the love she was getting after her journey back to the Olympics.

Finally, two names later, it was my turn. *From Vancouver, Washington, Jordan Chiiiiiiiles!* I ran out onto the floor, pulsing with energy. I even decided to give it a little extra— instead of just running out hands raised, I did a little dance for the crowd that ended in a Rosie the Riveter kind of flex. The cheers rocked the rafters. I was so pumped for this one! So energized to step into this meet.

We would each compete in all events both Friday and Sunday. Shilese sat out the vault rotation on day one before competing on uneven bars, then ended up withdrawing from the remainder of the night's competition because of her earlier injury—it turned out she had torn the ACL and meniscus in her left knee. Then Kayla DiCello, a two-time world medalist, performed her Yurchenko double full during floor and when she landed, her Achilles ruptured. She left the arena in a wheelchair and in tears. We all felt so bad for both of them. But you just have to keep going, knowing an injury could stop any one of us at any moment. That definitely adds to the tension in every competition.

After day one, I was in second place, behind Simone. The judges would take our scores from both competition days into account to determine who would be on Team USA at the Olympics, and I was feeling pretty good about going into day two in second.

"You know what we always say," I reminded Simone with a grin. "Let's just hit it like that tomorrow, and we're good. No pressure."

Saturday was mostly a day for relaxing: after a short practice I spent time with my family out and about in Minneapolis. The next morning, Simone and I woke up and looked at each other from across the aisle between our beds. First day, done. Let's get it.

She put on some Sexyy Red, up-tempo music that would get us energized to compete again. We vibed out as we got ready for the second day of Trials, and I was honestly struck by how much fun we were having getting ready. My nerves were gone. My worries about injuries had evaporated. Now I just wanted to go out there and give it my all.

When three o'clock rolled around and it was time to head out to the arena again, I grabbed my gym bag and my phone and we headed out the hotel room door. I Face-Timed my parents so that we could pray together. We got to the arena before the audience started filling the stands, and this time I stopped in my tracks to just take it in. The magnitude of it all. The weight of the moment that this could very well be my last run. For some of us, it would be.

*   *   *

We started that competition day on vault. Olympic order is always vault, bars, beam, floor. As you run down the eighty-two-foot runway toward a vault, the world blurs. All of the screams and shouts surrounding you run together into one thrilled roar that seems to help lift you into the air. A vault takes only about five or six seconds, from the moment you start your run to the second you raise your arms above your head in salute. In those seconds, I barely have time to think. There's no room in your head for anything but what you're doing, trying to stick the landing that will change your life. What we do is already scary—hurling ourselves to impossible heights, upside down and flipping through the air—so I don't want to psych myself out. I just tell myself, in the moment I salute the judges and step onto the runway, *All you have to do is land on your feet.*

I stuck my Yurchenko double full with a little more of a hop than I would have liked on the landing, but I was riding the high of the crowd, and I knew that it was still a good vault. As I awaited that score, my first score of the day, I clapped my hands in a rhythm and the sold-out crowd of sixteen thousand joined in. The rhinestones down the arms and torso of my red, white, and blue leo shimmered under the lights. Today's competition leo was blue on the bottom with blue-and-red ombre and crystal detailing down the long sleeves. I loved it.

Let's go, Jo! I heard members of the audience cheering me on, as we all awaited my score. I tried to remain focused on what was coming next, my second vault, but the show of appreciation did keep my momentum going. The score came back: *14.500*. Solid. It can be difficult for me to get good scores for my vault heights because the judges compare my heights and distance from the vault to those of the other, taller gymnasts. So I was satisfied with that score.

"Let's work! Let's work, Chick!" my parents screamed in the crowd, on their feet along with everyone else. My mom, dad, grandmas, grandpa, aunties, uncle, and my brother Ty all wore shirts that said, JORDAN CHILES IS THAT GIRL, which my mom designed and my father, who'd started a graphic design business, had made.

I took a deep breath and saluted for my second vault. I stuck my landing, clapping and giving myself a little shake of the fist in triumph. "She means business tonight," I later heard one of the commentators say about my day two vaults. They were right. But I never lost sight of the fact that it could have gone differently.

So far my day two scores were an improvement over day one's. As athletes, we're used to picking apart our performances even more viciously than the judges do at times, but I'd learned over the years to try to control only what I could control. This was a good start.

I jumped down off the mat and slapped high fives with Josc. *Only three more events to go*, I thought to myself.

*   *   *

I was the very last girl to perform my vault and the second girl in the first group to perform on bars. As I stepped up to the bars, Simone gave me a nod and a smile. It's our confirmation to each other, like, *You're good. Let's get it.*

I saluted and saw the judge raise her hand for me to

begin. Within seconds, I was swinging through the air in rhythm, like a superhero—that's how I like to think of it. It's a warm reminder to me of how far I've come, back from those days as a little girl who wanted nothing more than to be able to do just this.

On bars, I've had to practice when to breathe over the years because it's so difficult to breathe normally as you're swinging from bar to bar, trying to keep your form perfect and your routine flawless at the same time. It's all about endurance, and you have to find the rhythm of the routine to build in where it's best to take your breaths. "Maybe breathe on the cast handstand or on the giants," Simone once advised me. And I did.

The moment I landed, I knew it had been a good routine with only one missed connection. I slapped a high five with Coach Laurent and hopped off the mat, waiting for my score to come in.

14.200. I was happy with that.

*   *   *

Later that day, my momentum seemed to slow. I made mistakes that I knew I shouldn't have. I was the last one on beam, after being second on bars, so I had a long time in between events. I was lying around on couches and trying to stay connected. USAG had brought in couches instead of chairs, which was new, and we loved them. But maybe I lost some of my focus along the way. Maybe I wasn't wrapped tightly enough inside of my own bubble.

Simone, Suni, and I all fell on beam. Honestly, if there

was one event I could just delete from gymnastics, it would be beam. *Ooooooooh*, I heard the crowd groan as I struggled and failed to catch my balance before falling. When you fall off beam, it's the most devastating feeling in the world. It's like it happens in slow motion, a car wreck you can see coming but cannot stop. But then the cheers erupted again as I tossed my head back, holding it high, and jumped back on. I had a solid routine after I recovered and got back on the beam, but I was still frustrated with myself. I couldn't even muster a smile for the crowd as I jumped quickly off the podium and walked away from that event. I couldn't get away fast enough.

"It's okay! It's okay!" my mom screamed from the stands, still standing and clapping for me. But I didn't feel like it was okay. As a gymnast in competitions, even in your moments of frustration with yourself you can't scream or yell like you'd want to, kicking yourself for messing up, because you're still on. You're still on view for the world to see. You have to bottle up those emotions, pressing them back down deep, deep, until you get through the rest of your routine, stick your landing, and walk away from the event. All the while, you're hyperaware that you're being watched by thousands of people. Part of the performance is keeping it all together.

I didn't even want to look at my score from beam because I knew it was going to be awful. *Okay, do I cry now or later?* I asked myself as I flopped down on the couch. I was approaching the last event of the competition, my floor routine, possibly the last event of my year if I failed to make the team. Simone and I looked at each other as the other floor routines were already underway.

No, don't look at me, we both said silently. *We're going to end up crying. Don't do that. Don't do that.*

We both knew that the moment where we'd find out if I made the team was coming. Every sports commentator in the world expected Simone to be there, and she was at the top of the leaderboard. But I needed to pull it together, and *keep* it together. Another performance like that and I could kiss my dream goodbye.

I had some time to burn before my turn on floor. I went to retape my ankles. I always had to keep my bad Achilles tendons in mind and keep them taped so they wouldn't get damaged during my tumbling passes. As they were getting taped, I had time to sit and think about what had just happened on the beam. I had made a mistake, but I couldn't let it ruin the rest of my night. I still had another performance to go—and I still had a shot at my dream.

As the floor routines started, I shook off my somber mood and started hyping up the crowd, finding my way back to my old self again. I remembered the lessons of therapy. Remembered my parents' words: *Who are you?*

I'm Jordan Chiles. I'm that girl.

When it was Simone's turn for floor, I turned to her and asked, "What corner do you need me in?" In general, I try not to focus on anyone else's performances, not even my own teammates'. I don't want to get distracted by what everyone else is doing, and I like to cheer on the audience. But I always watch at least part of my teammates' events so I can cheer.

And that was our ritual for the floor routine, telling each other which corner we'd tumble and finish in, so that we could be the first one there to help each other remember to breathe, to cheer the other one on. Hyping each other up was an important part of our competition days, and today was no different, even with my devastating fall from the beam moments before. As her music and routine started, the opening electronica bass pulsing through the arena, I threw on my hoodie and zipped it up over my leo. Josc and I moved to one corner of the floor to cheer her on.

As Simone finished her routine and stepped off the floor, taking a seat with so many cameras pointed right in her face, I stepped up to give her a huge high five. "You did it, girl! That was amazing!" She was still catching her breath and I was emotional, thinking, *Oh my gosh, my bestie did it! I'm so proud of her!* She'd overcome so many obstacles to come back and conquer it all again, and it was really cool to be able to witness that firsthand.

Later, as I walked up the stairs to the floor to do my own routine, the emotions flooded back through me again. There's a picture of me looking up with my eyes closed before that routine, as I held back tears and struggled not to cry. In that moment, I was feeling my auntie and grandpa watching over me. *This is for you*, I told them. *This is for you.*

I stepped onto the floor, and it was Beyoncé time. I knew that hip-hop wasn't usually something an "elite" gymnast would use for their routines—like my hair, it didn't fit the old view of what gymnastics should be. But I didn't care anymore. I would be myself, no matter what anyone had to say about it. I went with my heart's desire: Queen Bey herself, the muse for that year's theme. Laurent and Cécile fully supported me in this. Artistic is artistic—I could choose to show my artistry through whatever music I chose.

The moment the medley came on, the crowd went crazy,

and that spurred me on. This time, Simone and Joscelyn were standing at a corner cheering *me* on, even shaking their heads and bouncing their shoulders along with me—we'd seen one another's routines so many times now.

As I prepared for my last tumbling pass, Simone was beating her fists against the stairs, cheering me on, putting her hands to her mouth to yell to me as loud as she could over the roar of the audience, "Come on! Come on! You got this, Jordan!"

As I started running into that tumbling pass, this was it. The adrenaline pumped through me, with the wind on my face as I flipped in the air. When I stuck the landing, the audience exploded in wild applause. And I couldn't hold it in anymore. When I finally let the emotions of the past few days—the past few years—flood through me, I broke down in tears right then and there, on camera for the world to see. *Jordan Chiles Finishes Floor Routine in Tears*, the headlines would read.

But when I hit that ending pose, my arms above my head, I knew I had done the hard part. I had conquered that mountain I'd set out to climb, no matter the outcome. Even if I didn't get chosen for the Olympic team, I had put it all out there on the floor and done everything I could. And I just knew that in this moment, right here, I was that girl.

17

DREAM TEAM

The Olympics selection process always feels like you're waiting for the Wizard of Oz to reveal himself from behind the curtain. The decision is out of your hands, and the ones deciding your fate are literally out of sight, behind closed doors.

After the meet ended, we all came together into a huddle. We high-fived and cheered for one another, with tears in our eyes. We all go into each competition cycle knowing that this *could* be our last one. Age or injuries might keep us from trying again, or regular life with college or families and kids . . . This was the end of the road for some and the start of a new road for others. Only we didn't yet know which road we'd be traveling.

I noticed that even Coach Laurent's eyes were wet. I'd never seen him that emotional before. He was always our rock and steady hand in the storm, but now even he felt overcome.

"Let's say 'go Team USA' on three!" Simone motivated us. "One, two, three!"

"GO TEAM USA!"

We screamed it as loud as we could, our voices rising over the excited noise of the audience. And then cries, literally sobbing. Suni, Simone, Jade, and I—I think we were the worst crybabies there in that huddle because, for us, our redemption from Tokyo was on the line. We wanted to come back and give it everything we had. We had all matured so much over the past few years, not only in our gymnastics but within ourselves as women. Simone and I finally allowed ourselves to give each other the emotional look we'd been holding back. Now we could let it all out.

We wrapped each other in the tightest hug. "I'm so proud of you," we told each other. And it couldn't have been truer. I knew that girl would forever be with me, no matter where I was at in life. She would always be right by my side, a true one for real.

But that moment together, there in that huddle, only lasted for an instant. Then we got swept up in the time crunch that is live TV. The selection committee has twenty minutes to select the Olympic team: the five core members plus two traveling alternates and two nontraveling alternates. The Target Center was still going wild, with cheers and fans screaming our names, but now it was time to learn our fates.

They shuffled the thirteen of us down an arena corridor and into a private suite that would usually function as a club lounge for season ticket holders or a Diamond Club.

It was set up like a restaurant, but we were the only ones in there. I couldn't just sit there waiting. I wanted to keep moving to keep my nerves down, so Simone and I went to change out of our competition leos and into our team sweatsuits.

When we came back, some of our coaches were sitting, some were standing, but everyone was so closely packed together that the large room felt empty around us. We gymnasts sat on a half-circle sofa, whispering to one another, *Oh my gosh. What's gonna happen? How are you feeling?* We sat huddled, hand in hand, waiting.

I'd managed to keep my nerves down until the moment the selection committee walked in. They took their places in front of our little couch area, and that's when I could feel us all shaking, the vibrations traveling through our sweaty hands from one to the next. The committee hadn't even taken the full twenty minutes that they were allotted. They'd come back in five to ten minutes, and I sat stunned, paralyzed for a second. *Wait, it's time already? Wow, it's time already . . .*

I'd already decided with my family that if I didn't make this team, I was going back to school at UCLA. But if I *did* make it, I had a whole other long but exciting journey ahead of me.

Alicia Sacramone Quinn, one of the members of the selection committee, smiled slightly and opened her mouth to speak. The room was hushed from the moment they'd walked in, and her words rang out clearly. "Congratulations to all of the girls. You guys did a remarkable job." Then she looked down at the paper in her hand and said the words we'd all been waiting for. I think I even stopped breathing for a second as I waited to hear what she'd say. "We're not going in any particular order, but we are going to announce who has made the Olympic team and who are the traveling alternates and nontraveling alternates."

It felt like she'd been talking for fifty minutes rather than fifty seconds. And when she started announcing the names, it was mine she called first.

"Jordan Chiles."

I remember thinking, *Thank you, God. Thank you.*

There was applause around the room, and my coaches hugged me as I stood to accept their embrace. There were so many things I wanted to say to them, to thank them for helping to get me to this moment—but at the very forefront of my mind was the thought: *Where is my phone? How do I call my parents?!* I knew they were bursting to find out the news, along with everyone else in the Target Center Arena, but there was no time to call them.

After my name, they called Jade Carey. Then Hezly Rivera. Then Suni Lee. Then Simone Biles. As they named the four alternates—Joscelyn Roberson and Leanne Wong as traveling alternates, and Kaliya Lincoln and Tiana Sumanasekera as nontraveling alternates—I was seriously buzzing with shock, and I broke down crying again. Four of us—Simone, Joscelyn, Tiana, and me—were from World Champions Centre. Even in the midst of my personal excitement, I also realized that this was historic. Our coaches had made history for themselves *and* for WCC—it was incredibly rare to have four athletes from one gym selected as part of an Olympic cycle.

But in the midst of so many happy tears and hugs and congratulations, there was also sadness and tears of disappointment from the girls who hadn't been chosen. The commotion took over and made everything a blur—a blur of triumph for some and regret for others.

Our team, it turned out, was the most decorated in USA Gymnastics Olympic Trials history. And we would soon find out that Cécile Canqueteau-Landi, our very own coach from World Champions Centre, had been named the coach of Team USA's women's gymnastics team.

But the audience and the cameras were expecting us in the arena, and now things had to move at breakneck speed. The lull of waiting was over. Now we would walk into the storm of media fire and expectations.

The five members of the team and the alternates were rushed through back halls of the arena and into another room, where Nike had set up shop. I had signed with them as one of my sponsors in the summer of 2023, and they were also brought on to dress the Olympic team. The door opened to a flurry of Nike reps and an entire dressing room, with a row of outfits hung on a rack and rows of white Nike sneakers. Internally, I screamed. Absolutely lost it. I'm such a fashion girl, with a wall of sneakers—including over fifty pairs of Jordans, my namesake—on display in my own bedroom, so this moment felt like its own kind of dream. Nike had hired designer Sami Miró, a former gymnast herself, to collaborate in the creation of our custom jackets.

We were told that Miró's custom design was inspired by the Greek goddess of victory herself, Nike. She wanted to give us a sense of confidence and strength as we walked out to greet the crowd, and she'd totally hit the mark. The clothes were all cream and white, with cream leather inlays and silk charmeuse fabric that felt so soft against my skin.

It felt rich. As they quickly handed me each piece of clothing, I thought to myself, *Oh, this goes perfect, and this goes perfect! It all looks so good together!*

Simone and I were laughing with each other. "Okay!" she whooped excitedly. "USA Gymnastics and Nike did the *big* one! They upped the scale, for real!"

It was really cool to have that moment with all the girls in that room, even as we were rushing around and only had about four minutes to get dressed. Now was when the bonding time between us really began. Now we were a team.

"Okay, guys, let's get a move on," I heard a voice call over the chaos. "TV's coming back. We have to go."

We finished tying our shoes and zipping up our jackets, and they ushered us out of that room and back toward the arena hall. We could hear the cheers of the fans even from where we were. I was disoriented at that point from having been rushed to so many different rooms; I had no idea where we actually were within the arena. They brought us into the backstage area, behind the megatron video screen, to the same tunnel we'd rushed out from to greet the crowd two days before, at the start of the competition.

Again, we lined up, and again, we waited for our names to be called, so that we could run out to the audience, who still had no idea who had made the team. Backstage, lined up, we joked and we cried. We took photos with one another on our phones and made little videos. Each of us was given a bouquet of cream and white flowers to take out with us as our names were announced.

"Jordan, you're up first," I was told.

"Wait, what? Why am *I* up first?"

"You're the hype woman for a reason," the person lining us up joked back. *Oh my gosh*, I thought with a laugh, *I'm gonna be boo-hooing all over the place. I'm not gonna be hyping up nobody!*

"Okay, thirty seconds and you guys are on!" they called out. It was crazy to think that less than ten minutes before, I'd been sitting on a couch with sweaty hands.

When my name was called—*Jordan Chiles!*—and I stepped out to the roar of the crowd, the moment overtook me. I crumbled, crouching down, crying. I finally felt wanted in this sport. And not just for what I could show but because of who I was, who I'd become. I could go to these Olympic Games and be the Jordan *I* wanted to be, I realized in that instant. Not the Jordan who was nineteen years old, trying to figure out what an Olympic Games was, but the Jordan that was twenty-three and had the ability to defend herself. Had the ability to speak from her heart—and the ability to speak her truth.

*   *   *

We called it the Redemption Tour.

Directly after the announcement of the 2024 women's Olympic gymnastics team at the Target Center Arena—and after I did gleeful snow angels, just like I did in Tokyo, in the shower of confetti raining down on us, for millions around the world to see—we had individual live-broadcast interviews with NBC on the floor of the arena. I got to run up to see my parents in the stands for a split second. I grabbed my mom's and dad's hands and we exchanged *I love you*s, then I took pictures and did a few TikToks with members of the crowd. I was having a ball. I handed my flowers to my UCLA head coach, Janelle McDonald, who was sitting near my family, and was ushered away, on to the next thing, again.

This time, it was Hoda Kotb and the *Today* show. Still in our cream team warm-ups, we were taken to a room that had been set up for a pretaped interview. It was the first of many team interviews that we would do in the next few days.

"I'm having a little weird déjà vu right now!" Hoda gushed at the start of our interview, referring to the fact that four of the five of us were repeat members of the US Olympic gymnastics team from Tokyo. Only Hezly Rivera, the baby of our squad, was a newcomer. She had just turned sixteen earlier that month and couldn't even really drive yet; we would often tease her. Hoda had always been a huge gymnastics fan, and TV coverage showed her cheering us on from the sidelines at the Olympic Trials. "Does it kind of feel like that? Does it feel like déjà vu for you, Simone?" she asked to kick us off.

"Déjà vu"—Simone nodded slightly, agreeing—"but also a little bit of a redemption tour." We all nodded in enthusiastic agreement. She'd hit the nail on the head. "I mean, in Tokyo, we all didn't have our best performances, so we're excited to go out there and kill it."

From then on, we would call it the Redemption Tour, both publicly and among ourselves. Silver was good, but we wanted that team gold in our hands.

After the interview with Hoda, we had several quick individual interviews in another room in the arena. The whole time, I was followed around by security guards and my USADA rep, as were all of the other members of the team. "I'm your USADA rep. Can you please sign this piece of paper?" she had asked me as we were on the move, as they always did, requesting that we acknowledge that they were there to drug test us. I signed, then kept it moving. As always, the USADA reps were there to monitor us before the drug test to ensure that we hadn't ingested anything we weren't supposed to, and we were not allowed to leave their sight at all. She had been walking around beside me since the moment I got announced on the Olympic team, like a shadow.

At this point, I really had to pee. We'd been nonstop since the end of the competition, and none of us could go to the restroom—not only because of the live TV time crunch but because we had drug testing scheduled for right after this. The USADA rep and I went into a private room in the arena for my drug test. The USADA process is complicated and detailed. If I took an Advil or a Zyrtec within the past seven days, I have to declare that in the system, just in case it pops up in my drug test.

She handed me the little box I'd become so familiar with by now, and I selected a pee cup and a lid. She watched me pee, which is the *most* uncomfortable part of the process. At twenty-three years old, someone was still watching me pee like I was a toddler. USADA maintained the right to test us at any time or location. After stepping off the podium and wanting to cheer and celebrate with your family . . . nope, drug test instead before you can. Once, when I was taking senior pictures at school, out in the forest, a USADA rep showed up—he'd gone to my house first and found out where I was. I had to pee and drug test right then, in an outhouse. It could happen at any time.

Ninety milliliters of liquid later, I signed my drug testing paperwork and went to find my family. They'd taken all of the families—team and alternates—as well as our sponsors to the Diamond Club area.

When I spotted my parents, I ran over and almost took my mom out, I hugged her so hard. "Ain't no way I just made another Olympic team!" I laughed in disbelief as they held me and told me, "You did it!" I burst into tears at the sight of them, now that I had a moment to slow down. Our families sacrifice so much when it comes to us playing sports at a high level. I thought back on the days when my parents used to alternate months with my uncle to be able to afford my gymnastics lessons. So I knew what my family had gone through. When I cried there in that suite with them, they cried too.

The families and athletes were surrounded by our USA Gymnastics reps, who also hugged us with congratulations. My Nike rep, Lori, was like, "Let's get this girl some food!" But we weren't going to eat there. Nike had something else in store for me.

We left the arena, and Lori put me and my parents into a waiting black car. It was around midnight by this point. The arena had cleared out, the fans gone home, and the night was dark around us, but we were being whisked away to somewhere else. We pulled up to a restaurant and walked in—and I saw that Nike, one of my biggest sponsors, had thrown a party just for me.

Oh my—what! I could smell pizza, fettuccine . . . I never eat before competitions because I don't want to feel heavy or weighed down. We hadn't had a moment to stop since the Trials were over. I hadn't eaten all day.

There were all of my Nike family, my uncle and auntie, my sisters and my brother Ty, my grandmas and grandpa, and two of my friends. They popped confetti over my head as I walked in, and I was completely floored. All of this, for *me*? I felt myself getting emotional again. All those tears all day, but I couldn't help it. Everyone in the room was cheering for *me*.

This was so much different from the lead-up to the Tokyo Olympics. Then, I was a nineteen-year-old girl following in Simone's twenty-three-year-old footsteps but not yet an established athlete myself. I didn't even have my own sponsors at that point. I just always joined in with whatever Simone had going on. And she let me. We had always been together, the two families, in full celebration mode, since I'd joined her gym in 2019. But this was the first time that I'd had an event thrown just for me.

*   *   *

After it was announced that I'd made the 2024 Olympic Team, I was surprised at the warm outpouring of love I received—not just from fans in my social media comments but from celebrities I'd looked up to for years. Megan Thee Stallion sent me flowers the size of the world, signed not with her full stage name but just *Megan*. I was so touched! Then, on July 9, I received the shock of my life when my namesake Michael Jordan himself sent me a congratulatory text. *Hey Jordan, this is Michael Jordan. I am so excited to watch you win a gold medal. Here's to wishing you nothing but good luck. Let's catch up afterward. Hope to see you soon. MJ.*

I nearly dropped my phone. *But how did he get my number?* I wondered. Could this be real? I texted my mom immediately, asking her if she'd given him my number and if she thought the text was real. She didn't know, but she hadn't given out my number. I reached out to my agents, my publicist. Nope and nope. *What in the world?* I was starting to feel disappointed, thinking, *This isn't really him.* The thought struck me that I'd have to change my number too. Someone was crank texting me! Then we were like, *Wait, hold up. We need to send this to Nike.* He had a long-standing relationship with them. They would be able to tell me if this was real.

It took what felt like a while to hear back. I even took a nap as I waited, then went back to the gym for my second practice of the day. But then I got a text from Nike that said it was really him. I texted him back, *OMG I have no words right now! I'm speechless and thank you very much. This is really crazy.* It felt completely unreal, that *I* was casually texting with this great man my mom had insisted I be named after. And we kept the conversation going for a while. *By the way, love the name,* he joked.

Later, at the Olympics, Snoop Dogg would bring it up to my mom. Word had somehow gotten around the grapevine. Snoop was like, "So, it's really true that Michael Jordan texted Jordan."

"Yeah, it was so cool!" my mom confirmed.

But no, she quickly realized, he wasn't asking her, he was telling her. He goes, "No, I'm telling you, it's really true. Because as soon as I heard about it, I was like, *I gotta verify this.* You know, like I gotta see if she's telling the truth or whatever! I just wanna let you know"—he laughed—"*I have never met Michael Jordan, and I'm Snoop Dogg!*"

Michael Jordan means so much to the Black community. I have admired everything from his famous "flu game" to his overall dedication to his sports and the devotion he showed to his family. When it comes to somebody who understands the sport and understands his culture and the game so well, it hit different for me. That's why I have always cherished his name so much.

But the embrace from my community didn't stop there. On July 17, Beyoncé sent me a handwritten note along with the *Cowboy Carter* album cover. I nearly keeled over in tears. *Congrats to you Queen*, the note read. *I always watch you with pride and admiration. Thank you for repping us. Good luck to you. All of your hard work and sacrifice shines bright. Praying for you and wishing you the best. Love, your twin Beyoncé.*

I'm not exaggerating when I say I could barely breathe. To see that one of my idols had not only watched my performances but thought enough of me to send me such a tremendously thoughtful gift—*and* call me "twin"? I pulled out my phone and immediately told the world the news. I couldn't hold it inside.

Ahhhhhhh!!! I'm screaming right now!! Yall @beyonce sent me this and I'm crying!!! I posted on Instagram with a photo of the cover she'd sent me. I learned that during the Olympic Trials, she and Jay-Z had been checking in on me with someone we knew in common to see how I was doing through it all. I felt such love from them, like big sis and big bro energy.

All of this felt so absolutely surreal to me. You have to understand, I'm a girl who still tells herself she's broken half the time. At that point, leading up to the Paris Olympics, I still hadn't gotten used to all the attention, and I certainly did not consider myself to be famous. I'd tried to lead as normal a life as possible outside of the gym and my sport, so this attention hit me with a flood of emotions. Before this, I felt like I wasn't being seen at all. I felt like I was just this little Black girl trying to fulfill something in her life but that my voice was being shut off. So feeling this love and acknowledgment of all my hard work from so many people renowned around the world was incredible. They'd taken time out of their lives to watch, and consider, and reach out to me, and that gave me a new level of confidence in myself.

18

BONJOUR PARIS

We had only two and a half weeks from the day we left Minneapolis to when we'd be boarding the plane for France and the Olympics. We spent that time training (of course), first in our home gyms with our own coaches, then all together at prep camp in Katy, Texas. I could just drive there since Katy is only forty-five minutes from my home gym.

Olympic prep camp is three days long. It's a time for team bonding because we come from different gyms across the nation and most of us don't train together. Suni was from Minnesota. Jade had come in from Oregon, where she went to college at Oregon State, and Hezly was from the Dallas area. Cécile had been named our team's head coach, but each of the gymnasts brought their own coaches as well. Laurent was there in his capacity as a coach to both Simone and me.

A week or so after Trials, my former Tokyo Olympics teammate MyKayla Skinner went viral for saying the "talent and the depth just isn't what it used to be" on Team USA. She said that apart from Simone, "a lot of girls don't work as hard" and "just don't have the work ethic." *Yeah, okay.* Her comments barely registered in my mind; I'd been through so much in the sport that her words just felt laughable and bitter. They echoed all the sentiments I'd heard before about gymnasts of color from white gymnasts. Five out of the seven of us who traveled to the Olympics were girls of color—and, of course, she could never say that Simone, the most decorated gymnast of all time, didn't work hard. Internally, Team USA started calling ourselves FAAFO, *f--- around and find out,* as a humorous nod toward her words. We knew how hard we'd worked and that we had it in us to bring home the gold.

After prep camp, we all flew together on July 18 out of Bush Intercontinental Airport in Houston. We had a layover in Atlanta, and we almost missed our flight to France due to weather issues, but they held the plane for us. I was honored that the airport and airline would do that for the Olympic team. After our layover in Atlanta, I slept for the entire rest of the flight.

Before Paris, we headed to the north of France for another training camp. We would stay there for four days before moving into the Olympic Village. Team USA athletes often train somewhere else before settling in at our actual training facilities for the Olympics—it helps us acclimate and get used to the time zone change before the intensity of the Village. The men's basketball team went to London, for example.

We trained at a facility called AMGA Gymnastique, in Arques, France, and it was all vibes. Luckily, this time would not be like last time—we could all train together without the fear of being sent home hovering over our heads, like it did when we were in Tokyo. We still had plenty to worry about, though. It's a rare occurrence, but we could be switched out for an alternate anytime during the weeks leading up to the Olympics Podium Training, based on how we looked in practice. The possibility of injury also always loomed. We had to bring our best to the floor every single day, because anything could happen.

*   *   *

When we got to the Olympic Village, things got real, fast. We hadn't gotten the full Olympic experience in Tokyo at all, so I was excited to finally have it in Paris. The minute we got off the bus going into the Village, I was scream-ing—no, literally, screaming. There was so much hustle and bustle as whole Olympic teams got situated, stepping off of shuttles, finding their way to their apartments, and no one even batted an eye when I screamed, "Oh my gosh, we're here!" A large *Paris 2024* banner greeted us at the entryway to the Village. In the Olympic Village, every-body loves the gymnasts—that's what Simone told me as we walked along, accepting waves from people we didn't even know and waving back. I felt the pressure of this in an unexpected way. Just walking through the Village, being ourselves, we were recognized, especially Simone.

Our bags were dropped where we'd be staying, and we athletes were taken straight from the bus to our Team USA experience at an Olympic content creator house, where we were given our Olympic gear in what's called "team kits." Many of us had corporate sponsorships, and every Team USA sponsor we had sent us tons of gear, paraphernalia, and new apparel for us to try on, wear, and create content for in the content creator house. This was an amazing honor because we got access to items the greater public didn't have yet, so that we could create branded content for our sponsors to promote it and us.

Even our team kits, which everyone on the team received, were kept very secret until they were given to us because they were filled with stuff that consumers wouldn't be able to buy until it officially came out. We were loaded up with dope Nike gear and sneakers. We were in the content creator house for hours, just trying on new stuff and posting TikTok videos together. There was also Hershey's, Omega, and Fenty sponsorship merch there, among others, for Team USA athletes for various sports.

From there, we went through the accreditation process. The Olympic Village isn't just open to anyone—even my own mom couldn't walk into the Village to give Suni and me Cheetos hot fries she'd brought from the US; a USAG staff member at her hotel had to deliver it to one of my coaches, who'd meet them outside the Village. So, at accreditation, our passports were scanned, and we were given credentials that would allow us on and off the Village campus. The security was the tightest I'd ever seen anywhere in my life, but that added to the thrilling feeling of *I've made it!* I was finally one of the elite group who got to live through this experience—and I'd worked my butt off to get here.

*   *   *

Our Team USA apartment was amazing (well, except for the cardboard beds). It was on the fourth floor of the apartment building that would hold all of the Olympians competing for the US. The alternates didn't stay with us; there was an alternate Olympic Village on a different campus for the alternates from every country. "Yo, there's no way we are here at this moment!" I said when we walked up to our building. "You all remember where we were four years ago?" And everybody just started laughing. I was like, "No, I'm being serious. Like, yo, we are standing in front of our Team USA house." It was this big building that looked like we were in New York City.

In our team apartment, Jade and Simone roomed together, Suni and I roomed together, and Hezly was given her own room because she was the youngest.

Suni and I had grown close in the time between Tokyo and Paris. Not only were we now both repeat Olympians, but we'd had so many intimate conversations as she'd battled not one but two different forms of kidney disease. Though we were from separate gyms in different parts of the country, I knew that she'd spent four whole months out of the gym in 2023, and that the medication she'd taken for her kidney disease had left her hands so swollen that they wouldn't fit into the grips for her to train. She was often nauseated, and there were mornings where she couldn't even get out of bed. She'd had to fight to make it back to the Olympics. She too had broken down in tears at the end of Trials. She had been battling constant self-doubt, and the crushing weight of now being a celebrity on top of it all. We'd been able to lean on each other, to help each other stay motivated, communicating by phone and text. We both knew what it was like to find ourselves not in the best mental state of mind, and we could buoy each other up through it all, knowing so intimately the exact challenges that we faced as members of an Olympic gymnastics team. I love her to death and I'm very, very proud of her. I looked forward to sharing a room with her.

From the time we first arrived in the Village, our mornings were chaotic to say the least. Imagine five young women trying to get ready in just two bathrooms. But times like that made us all feel so close. The apartment felt like a safe space away from the cameras and judges, a place where we could just . . . *be*. And Simone always came through with the music, turning up her playlist so we could vibe out as we got ready.

Two days after we arrived at the Olympic Village, it was the morning of Podium Training, and it started off with a bang. As we all knew, Podium is where the Olympics really begins for gymnasts. This is where we would start being judged and where we had to perform everything full-out before the actual competition the next day.

Suni is always so hard to wake up in the mornings, and we laughed about how her alarm went off five times before she finally dragged herself out of bed.

"Suni, turn *off* your alarm!" I yelled at her playfully around nine a.m. "Come on now, it's time to get *up!*"

As she and Hezly went down to breakfast in the Olympic Village cafeteria (which was basically a food court with cuisine from around the world), I found myself sitting on my bed, trying to stay relaxed. I didn't want to get my nerves all worked up and psych myself out. Three days after Podium would be Qualifications—and that was the make-or-break moment when we would find out what events we would each be competing in for Team USA and whether or not we would make all-around, and the chance to earn individual apparatus medals for ourselves. At the Olympics, we're selected for the all-around based on our overall scores in the qualification round. The twenty-four gymnasts with the highest scores advance to the all-around final, but there's a maximum of two gymnasts per country who can go. That means that even if every core member of Team USA ranked higher than the other countries' gymnasts' highest scores, we could still only send two to compete in the all-around final. The gymnast with the highest cumulative score across all apparatuses wins the individual gold medal. It's complicated, but after all these years we totally knew the drill—and the stakes.

I had never performed in an all-around or any individual apparatus final at the Olympics before, and I'd be lying if I said I didn't want it desperately. The chance to earn my own medal, in addition to helping Team USA get gold, would mean everything to me. Because we all knew how serious today could be for each of us, there was very little conversation going on in the apartment that morning before Podium. We knew that it was almost time to suit up for real now, and we all separately went through our own personal rituals of getting in that mindset.

I was almost always the last one ready to walk out the door because I was always running around helping everyone else get ready, braiding hair and helping with leos. In fact, I'd stayed up until around midnight braiding everyone's hair the night before, so we all had braids up the middle with our hair pulled into buns. Pop and R & B—from Victoria Monét to Drake, Beyoncé to Latto—filled the room as we raced around. I did my makeup in the mirror. I didn't want to put on too extravagant a face for Podium. Save that for the big show. So I kept it simple with foundation, concealer, a nice blush, and some mascara. Today's leo was inspired by fireworks. I put mine in my gym bag, and I was ready to hit the arena.

We all got on the elevator and walked down to the bus, each listening to our music and getting in the mindset to show what we had at Podium. If I had to use one word to describe our vibe going onto that bus, that word would be *determined*. After all, it was the Redemption Tour for four of us, and it was Hezly's first time ever at the Olympics.

It was about a forty-five-minute drive from the Olympic Village apartments to the arena. On the bus with us were the gymnastics teams from China and Italy. Who would be on our bus ride to Podium was determined by a random draw, made earlier in the Olympic year, for our country's "subdivisions" for each sport.

The Olympic gymnastics teams are broken up into eight subdivisions; each subdivision is composed of two to four teams. That way, we're not all heading to the arena for Podium at the same time, but, more importantly, this random draw determines what order each country will compete in for Qualifications the following day. For example, subdivisions one and two competed for Qualifications in the first two sessions of the day. Then subdivisions three and four, and so forth. This is significant because your subdivision determines how long you have to wait to compete that day for Quals. It's an unspoken but known fact that you want to get drawn to compete *later* in the draw, but we were early, subdivision two. That meant we'd compete as one of the first teams and then have to wait until the very last session was done to find out if we qualified to team finals. That anticipation of waiting is so nerve-racking.

Gymnastics involves a certain level of subjectivity because we're judged by human beings, and everything is based off the scores the judges give us. Sometimes the judges are tighter—more nitpicky—with their judging at the beginning of Qualifications, and then they're looser with it toward the end. That's another reason teams prefer to compete later. You also want to go later on in sessions because this determines the individual events that you make as well. There's the all-around, vault final, beam final, floor final, and bars final. Qualifications is where you qualify to those particular events. So if the judges are judging tight at the beginning of the subdivisions, you don't know if they're going to score you the same as they would score somebody going in the later evening session. They should, but they don't always.

Going later in the subdivisions also means that most of the other countries' scores are already set, so you know exactly what you have to do, what scores you need to get, in order to be one of the only eight teams from around the world who will ultimately qualify to compete in the team final, rather than having to wait around to see how your scores will stack up against everyone else's as an earlier subdivision competitor. But because Team USA has historically been one of the best in the world, especially in recent

Olympic cycles, we know that if we just go in there and hit our routines, we'll qualify to team finals.

As we got on the bus to head to Podium, we found that most of the seats had already been taken. Sometimes this happens, depending on how many people from each team get on the bus—including the coaches, trainers, and coordinators each team brings. Typically, the coaches and coordinators give up their seats for athletes as a show of goodwill, sportsmanship, and respect. When we saw that most of the seats had been taken, Simone politely asked a trainer from one of the other teams if they would give up their seat so I could sit there. Otherwise, I'd end up standing all the way to the arena, forty-five minutes away, on an un-air-conditioned bus, right before having to compete for Qualifications. He yelled at her, going on about his federation and how he had the right to be there too. In my head, I thought to myself, *Ummm, okay, that didn't go as I thought it would. You're not the one competing, but . . . okay, all good.* Outwardly, I just looked at him and was like, "Can I sit down, please?"

Surprisingly, he then said, "Yeah, since *you* asked me, unlike your teammate."

"Well, my teammate did ask you. She was asking for *me*, but okay," I said as he finally stood, and I sat down.

Because of the lack of AC—which seemed crazy given that this was a bus full of athletes on the way to the biggest competition stage on the planet—we were all sweating by the time we arrived at Bercy Arena. At the arena, there were two different areas: the training hall, called the back gym, and the arena itself. Teams USA, China, and Italy all warmed up together in the back gym, as is customary; you warm up for Podium with the teams in your subdivision. There's typically little interaction among teams because you're trying to get your game face on for competition, so I didn't have to have any dealings with that trainer from the other team again.

Teams warm up on the second event that they're competing in, then work their way through the rest of the events. That way, your last event that you're warming up on is the first event that you're actually competing in—ensuring that you're as ready as you can be for your first event. Our team warmed up on floor first, then vault, bars, and beam. I felt ready for what was to come as the Olympic arena volunteers reminded us of the rules of Olympic Podium: *Make sure you're lined up in order because they'll call your names for introductions in order; you can only have a certain amount of coaches on the competition floor at a time; do not wear dangly earrings. If you're wearing some, please remove them. And do not rotate to the next event until your volunteer comes to lead you to the next event, or you'll have points deducted from your team.* Here, like at the Podium for Olympic Trials, we would go through a mock competition and receive mock scores.

I performed well on all of my events, and we all felt confident going into Qualifications the next day. By the time we got back to the Village, it was eight o'clock at night. The Olympic Village was its own self-sustaining campus, with grab-and-gos where you could get ready-made food, yogurts, and other handheld snacks without the exchange of money—just grab and go. And there were grocery stores full of nutritious foods—but we just wanted something hot and easy after that long day at Podium. Simone and I didn't really like the dining hall food—I was never able to find anything there that actually tasted good. As we got off the bus, I turned to her and said, "Okay, I know we don't like the food, but can we at least get the pizza?" We needed *something* to hold us over until the next day.

As we were in line for pizza, we met Shelly-Ann Fraser-Pryce, the track and field star from Jamaica. It was like we'd summoned her or something—it was the funniest thing. We had just been talking about the *Sprint* documentary, which was being filmed to give a behind-the-scenes look at the track and field athletes and races at the Olympic Games. It would be part of a Netflix series that had started earlier that month, featuring the 2023 Diamond League and World Athletics Championships leading up to the Olympics.

"Have you started watching the series?" Simone asked me.

"No, I haven't seen it yet, but I wonder how they're going to film stuff like that here—for your documentary too— you know, as people are competing." Netflix had been following Simone around for months for her *Simone Biles Rising* documentary, and they would be there to film her at the Olympics as well.

Right then I looked over my shoulder and there was Shelly-Ann. I could tell it was her even though she was incognito, dressed down and with her hair covered up.

"Oh my gosh, Simone! There's Shelly-Ann Fraser-Pryce right *there*! Why don't we just ask her?" We were starstruck. Simone was even nervous to go over and speak to her.

"No, no, no," she insisted as I tried to push her toward Shelly-Ann.

"Don't you want to meet her? Come on; I met her at a shoot that I had a while back."

"Oh my gosh, Jordan, no!" Simone said as I went over to Shelly-Ann like a playful schoolgirl.

"My friend wants to meet you," I told her. Shelly-Ann recognized me and smiled, then looked over my shoulder at Simone. *That's* my friend? "Oh, wow, I *totally* know who she is," Shelly-Ann said. Everyone on that campus knew who Simone was, even if they were too shy to come up to her.

In the Olympic Village, there's a tradition where athletes can trade pins. Each team from each country is given a handful of pins that symbolize their team. We keep them on our lanyard badges, and as you meet other athletes, you can trade pins as a sign of friendship and to collect memorabilia from your encounters with one another.

"Do you wanna trade pins with us?" I asked Shelly-Ann. And we did. It was such a cool moment to be in the presence of two GOATs in their respective fields at the same time—and to see how they both recognized each other immediately, even without having met before.

Throughout our two and a half weeks in the Olympic Village, we met so many other athletes this way, including Coco Gauff from tennis—who already knew Suni—and Allyson Felix from track and field, who Simone had done sponsorship campaigns with. As we saw people we knew, we'd just go up to them and introduce our teammates.

But after a while, Simone and I stopped going outside to walk around the Village. There were so many people who immediately recognized her and asked to take pictures with her that it started triggering her anxiety. She could only say, "No, thank you," so many times without seeming rude, so we stayed in the apartment to protect her mental health and mine.

19

WORKING IT THROUGH

The morning of Qualifications was a Sunday. I woke up around nine a.m. By now, we were all familiar with the Village layout, and everybody dispersed in their own way, going to breakfast and such. Jade Carey had a stomach virus and had been vomiting; she'd been moved out of the apartment to recuperate so the rest of us wouldn't get sick too. So, that morning, it was just me, Hez, Suni, and Simone getting ready together, Simone's music blasting once again.

That day, I jazzed up my look a bit, using a glitter paste as eye shadow, so that my eyes would pop more, and I used eyeliner to create a cat eye. I slicked my hair into a low bun with a middle part with a bow in my hair.

On the way down the elevator to our bus, the four of us posed in the mirrored doors and had an *Are you ready? Ready!* moment. On the bus, I FaceTimed my parents so that they could pray with me. "Please send angels to protect her throughout the whole competition," my dad prayed, "and all of the girls on the competition floor. Please help her to do her best and forget the rest, to go out there and just have fun." He always prays for my protection and to keep me happy, healthy, and in one piece.

These Qualifications were huge for me. My Quals in Tokyo had been a disaster, and I wanted to show the world what I was truly capable of. I wanted a shot at an individual final as well as the overall team redemption of getting gold. As we changed into our spangled slate leos at the arena, the team as a whole seemed pumped and ready to go—we felt like we were about to take on the world.

We warmed up until it was time for lineup. I reveled in the roar of the crowd, as I always did. We would each perform one routine per event, except for vault, where some of us would perform two.

The arena was packed with people from around the world who wanted to watch our qualification round. Tom Cruise was there, Ariana Grande, Sarah Jessica Parker, and Matthew Broderick. Snoop Dog was sitting next to my parents! My mom told me later that Snoop was chatting with them the whole time, one hundred percent engaged and asking questions. She gets so nervous any time I perform, and talking to Snoop helped distract her and calm her nerves.

For Paris Qualifications, we did what's called "Four Up Three Count." That means that four out of five of us gymnasts perform on each event, and of those four, the three highest-ranking scores get counted toward the total team score. In Olympic Qualifications, you're trying to qualify the whole team to be able to compete for a medal; that's the first priority. The second priority at Qualifications is for each of us *individually* to qualify on each event final, as well as for the all-around final. So here, in Qualifications, you're hoping that you perform well enough that your team will want to use you for all-around, meaning competing in all of the four events, because that gives you an all-around score that can advance you to the all-around final, which is reserved for the top two members of the team for each country.

I wanted to be in that top two.

At Qualifications, we have been told by the head coach who will compete on each event. Simone, Suni, and I would be competing in all four events; Hezly and Jade would each compete in two. We just go out there and give it our all in the hopes of scoring well enough to qualify to an event final. In our minds, we gymnasts know what we're strongest in. Floor and vault were my top events as an athlete; Suni's were bars and beam. But there's still always a chance that any one of us could perform well enough in all of the events to qualify.

We started on beam, which is always the scariest thing in the entire universe. My overall start value on that event is lower than the other girls' on the team, but I was clean that day and landed a solid beam score. As a first-time Olympian, Hezly struggled with nerves during her beam routine. But we work as a team, so Simone's, Suni's, and my scores were the three scores that counted. Floor came next. Right before I stepped onto the mat I saw that Snoop was sitting next to my parents, so I waved and he did a little dance, and I danced back. No big deal, just me and Uncle Snoop breaking out some moves before an Olympic qualification event! I really wanted to qualify for the individual final on floor, and I was happy with my performance. Vault was easy. And then bars, which used to be so hard for me as a baby gymnast but have become one of my stronger events. I swung some beautiful bars that day, if I do say so myself, and when I landed I just screamed. Whatever came next, I knew I had redeemed myself.

What did come brought up complicated emotions. Since Tokyo, Suni and I had been alternating who scored better in the all-around. Going into her bar routine at Qualifications, she needed higher than a *14.799* to beat me out for second in the all-around. Her routine needed to be perfect in order to edge me out . . . and it was. She finished with a *14.866*, less than a tenth of a point above my score. I'd lost out in the margin of a pointed toe or a step on a landing, something that small.

I had a sinking feeling in my gut once they posted Suni's scores. Even televised, you could see the emotion on my face at the kiss and cry. Disappointment. The cameras zoomed right in on me, waiting for my reaction. Later some people on social media complained that I should have looked happier for my teammate. I *was* happy for her, but also sad for myself. Like anyone would be. Suni and I ended up posting a TikTok together showing the haters that we were good.

After all of us had competed, we headed home. At that point we were in first place in our subdivision, with Italy in second. Back at the apartment, Simone and I watched all of the other subdivisions compete throughout the day. *Okay, we're good,* we said as team after team performed. We were watching to see if anyone would surpass Team USA in the rankings, since we had gone early—subdivision two out of eight. As long as we stayed in the top eight, we would make the team final.

At the end of the night, Team USA was still at the top of the leaderboard—and by a good margin. For me, this was the first moment of redemption that I was looking for. Individually, Simone, Suni, and I were in the first, second, and third spots, all the way until the very last qualification group performed, so Team USA held all of the top three spots. In that last qualification group, Brazil's Rebeca Andrade—a huge talent and someone I have great respect for—scored well, so I finished Qualifications in fourth place overall. Simone finished first with a dominant score of *59.566*. Rebeca finished second with a score of *57.700*. Suni finished third with a score of *56.132*, and I came in fourth with an all-around score of *56.065*. Unfortunately, because of the two per country rule, I would not be able to compete in the all-around. Through all eight subdivisions of countries, Team USA had taken three of the top four spots—and my roommate and friend, Suni, had beaten me out by a sliver for the all-around final.

That night, we each individually found out what events we would compete in to represent Team USA for individual medals. I was doing floor; Suni was doing bars, beam, and all-around. Jade was doing vault, and Simone was doing all-around and every event except for bars.

That night, I was juggling so many emotions. I was crushed that I hadn't made it to the all-around final, even as I wanted to be happy for Suni that she had. I just wasn't ready to talk about it yet. Frankly, I was mad, and I ignored everybody for a few hours until I could pull myself together. Suni and I had had so many conversations over the years as we encouraged each other through our mental and physical hurdles. I knew what she had been through with her illnesses and that her health was why she hadn't been able to train as much as the rest of us. But I needed to sit with myself to process it. I remembered that my parents had always raised me to be a good human first. Whatever happened in gymnastics, it was most important that I hold my head high and be a good person.

I talked it all through with Simone in the apartment, venting all of my frustrations. Though I'd tried to hide it, Suni knew that I was disappointed, and she didn't come home to the apartment for a while, giving me space. She hung out with her family.

*   *   *

The day after Qualifications was a Monday. We had that day off and I just chilled in the apartment, trying to get my head together. I'd worked through my feelings enough to have gone to bed in the room Suni and I shared without tension on my mind, but it was still clear that something needed to be said between us.

The mental game of the Olympics was starting to affect all of us. We were getting tired, mentally and physically. We needed to make sure that the team remained solid, that we were going out there to compete the next day with one mind, all else aside.

On the eve of the women's gymnastics team finals, as Suni and I lay in our beds in the darkness, I let the silence stretch for a few minutes before I finally spoke. "Are you okay?"

"Yeah, I'm fine," she replied—although I wasn't sure it was true. Then she followed up with "I just didn't know if you're okay." Because I wasn't talking to her. I still hadn't really spoken to her much since that disappointing moment when her scores edged out mine—I just hadn't been ready. And now, even as I wanted to talk to her, I didn't know what to say or how to say it—and neither did she.

"Look, let's just stop this right here. I need to go get Simone to help with this," I told her. "I'll be right back."

"No," she protested as I climbed out of bed.

But I wasn't having it. "No, we're figuring this out now. I'm not going to bed like this. We're going to figure this out."

I called Simone into the room. Simone sat on the edge of my bed, and the words slowly started to come. The lights were off, and the darkness helped, honestly. We couldn't really see each other's faces, and that made it easier to talk without feeling judged.

"Okay, I don't know where everybody's at, but we're just going to talk real quick," I started. "Let's figure this out. Let's just put everything on the table because we have to come as a team tomorrow and dominate in what we do best."

Simone asked Suni if anything was on her mind, and Suni finally responded something like, "I don't understand how you guys are who you are." Simone and I had been a duo since before Tokyo, and we always had each other's backs. Biles and Chiles, as countless news articles, T-shirts, and fans' signs had proclaimed. To the other girls on the team, this might have felt intimidating, as we would always back each other up. For the last two Olympic cycles, two of the girls on a team so small had been a package deal. Maybe we'd realized this for a while now, but we'd never had a conversation like this where it was brought up. "How do you guys do it?" Suni wanted to know.

We explained to her that, yes, we were friends, but we all needed to be able to lean on each other, to support each other equally, if we wanted to be the best team that we could be. "Suni, me and Simone don't want you guys to feel no type of way about us always being together. We're a team, and none of us are here to tear anybody down, not one bit," I told her. Simone added, "We're not here to take away anything from you, or make you feel like your voice isn't heard. We know who you are, Suni, and we're here for you. We're a team, on and off the floor."

At that moment, at the Olympics, I was fully conscious that my safe space was Simone. But if we could all find that safe space in one another, then I knew we'd be all right.

Suni smiled at these words, and I felt some of the tension evaporate between us. She went on to talk about how the weight and expectations of the world's eyes had been triggering her self-doubt more and more, even now that she'd hit her goal of making it back to the Olympics, making it past her illnesses, which had kept her out of the gym for months. We told her that it was okay to take time for herself for her own mental health, that it was okay to say no to celebrity obligations when she needed her own space to think.

Simone was there to guide us through the conversation, asking us to go deeper, asking what we meant when we said this or that. At twenty-seven, she'd been through so much of this herself.

We all had so much within ourselves that we needed to overcome—Suni's self-doubts after her illnesses, my disappointment at not making the all-around final after all the hard work I'd put in. In our conversation that night, I realized that I needed to set my own disappointment aside and root for this girl who had been my friend and teammate for years. I genuinely *didn't* want to take anything from her, and seeing her in that vulnerable moment just brought me back to myself, reminding me of that. "Girl, you did your thing out there. I'm proud of you," I told her.

In being there for each other and admitting to her that I *was* proud of her for her performance, after she'd gone through so much especially, we were able to squash some things, figure things out. And we needed that going into the next day.

20

NOW YOU SEE IT, NOW YOU DON'T

The women's gymnastics team finals started the next morning. When I woke up, I felt calm and relaxed. Today was redemption day! I wasn't the same Jordan I'd been heading into the Tokyo team final, and I was eager to show the world how much I'd grown. Internalizing what my parents always told me—*Gymnastics is what you do, not who you are*—had freed me in so many ways. I would do my best for Team USA today, and no matter what happened, that would be more than enough. On the bus to the arena I called my parents, like always, and we prayed. The pressure and expectations were there, but I just felt peace.

Because we'd finished Quals in first place, Team USA was favored to win gold. As we ran out to greet the spectators, the applause was deafening, and I loved every moment.

The support took my hype level up several notches—exactly where I needed to be. Simone and I would do all four events, Suni every event except vault, which was Jade's only event. Newbie Hezly wouldn't participate this time, but she was only sixteen—her day would come.

And then it was go time! I started off our Redemption Tour with a powerful vault. Commentators often called me a "machine" on this event because vault came easy to me. That power made me rebound back a bit, but it felt great in the air. Jade and Simone went next and both were incredible—Jade in spite of that stomach bug. One down, three to go.

As I got ready to mount the bars, I heard my dad scream, "*Let's work!*" And I did. Bars were smooth and floaty for me and it was the same for Simone. Suni, after having faced so many medical issues, smashed her bar routine and walked off with a smile as wide as I've ever seen.

I was a little nervous heading into beam because . . . it's beam! I was off balance going into my front pike mount, and I fell off. My heart sank—oh no, not here!—but I pulled it together, as you have to, and made sure the rest was as close to perfect as I could get it. I finished strong and stuck my double pike dismount cold. There was no time to be upset—I had to cheer on Suni and Simone, who nailed their routines. I could feel the energy building in the arena. We all killed it that day, in each of our events, and by the time of our last event, floor, the crowd was so with us.

I wish I could tell you every detail of every moment that day, but my emotions were at an all-time high. I was on the cusp of achieving what I'd dreamed of since childhood. I remembered back to my eight-year-old self telling my family they should address me only as "Jordan Lucella Elizabeth Olympic Gold Medalist Chiles." Crazy thing is, I was serious. Even crazier, they went along with it (for a while!). When I finished the final pass of my floor routine and had given everything I had, I broke.

It was clear even before Simone's floor score went up that we would be taking home gold, but there's nothing like seeing it flash up on the Jumbotron. All five of us screamed and jumped up and down. We won by a wide margin, with a final overall score of *171.296*, 5.802 points above Italy's second-place and 6.799 above third-place Brazil. It was beyond thrilling to finally achieve the redemption we'd been seeking. We rushed the podium floor holding the American flag and waving to the cheering crowd. I looked up to my family and saw them all jumping and screaming too.

Before the medal ceremony, we went back to change. What no one but my family knew was that I'd had diamond and gold tooth grillz made just in case this moment manifested. I was going back and forth about wearing them, knowing it would be unfamiliar and maybe unacceptable to the elite gymnastics world, but my grillz screamed authentic to me and I decided to put them in. So there I was, listening to our national anthem, holding a gold medal and smiling wide with my grillz. I felt free to express myself no matter what others thought of it.

Later, Simone posted a photo on Instagram of the five of us holding the American flag, screaming with joy. The caption read: *lack of talent, lazy, olympic champions.* We also publicly revealed the team name that Cécile had come up with to help inspire us: "Golden Girls." It was perfect because we'd believed we would be gold medal winners, *and* we had the oldest team in US women's Olympic gymnastics since 1952: I was twenty-three, Simone twenty-seven, Jade twenty-four, and Suni twenty-one. Plus, we were iconic, just like the original Golden Girls on the TV show!

There was a party after our team win at a restaurant near the Olympic venue. Our families and friends were waiting for us there for quite a while, since we had to talk to the media and then get drug tested. A fun fact: peeing into a cup isn't so easy when you've been sweating as much as we just had. But we finally arrived, to the cheers and embraces of our loved ones, and it was worth the wait. I ran straight to my mom and practically knocked her over with my hug, then my dad pulled me into his chest. "I'm humbled to be her dad," he told people. We rocked out to "We Are the Champions" and "Party in the USA" and I let everyone hold my gold medal—which is heavier than you'd think. That night just might be the most fun I've ever had.

But our Olympic journey wasn't over yet. August 5 was the day I'd been waiting for. The individual gymnastics floor final, where I would be performing my routine in the hopes of winning my own individual medal for the very first time. I hadn't had the opportunity to perform an event final in Tokyo, so here was my moment.

Five minutes before I went out to perform the floor routine that would change my life and spark global controversy, I was honestly just relaxing. I went to the bathroom and put on some perfume. I touched up my makeup and smoothed down my hair. But when I got out into the arena for that final performance, the roar of the crowd shook me a bit deeper than it ever had before—in a good way. The lights felt like they'd gotten bigger. *Jordan, the lights are fine*, I told myself. *Nothing is different. You know how to do this.*

I was the very last person to perform my floor routine that night, ninth out of nine. Typically, there are only eight people, but that year, Rina Kishi of Japan and Ana Bărbosu of Romania were tied in qualifying scores for the women's floor final, which allowed nine gymnasts to advance to the final round. I was last to perform my routine at the floor final.

I wore a white leo studded with Swarovski crystals. I would later see that, when I made my entrance to start my routine, an NBC Sports broadcaster said, "Such a fun floor routine to end on!" I've always found those words so ironic because of what would come after.

When they called my name and I stepped onto that competition floor, everything became a blur. I had done this routine so many times throughout the year—hundreds of times between practice, warm-ups, and performances—but this was the big one. I really hadn't felt nervous during any of the other events, but now my heart was pounding. It was the final night, I was closing out the women's gymnastics events at the Paris Olympics, and so much was at stake. *Just stay on your feet*, I told myself as the music started and Beyoncé's voice filled my ears over the screams of the crowd. I knew this was the moment to put all of my very best work into what I'd been doing for my entire life. So many moments had felt like *the* moment. This one really was.

I stepped into the moves I'd come to know like the back of my hand. After a little hop on the landing at the end of my first tumbling pass, I recovered and really got into the routine—and the crowd could tell. Halfway through, the audience started to clap rhythmically to the beat, getting into it with me. In my final tumbling pass, I stung my ankles on the double layout landing; when you land short, it shoots this sharp pain up your legs. I finished the floor routine, and the crowd went crazy. As I walked off the floor, I couldn't even feel my ankles.

But that didn't matter. I'd given it everything I had.

*   *   *

As the world knows, my performance won me the bronze medal that night—after Coach Cécile made a successful inquiry into my initial score. Cécile's inquiry charged that the tour jeté full leap I had done hadn't been properly credited, and after looking at the video of my performance the judges agreed. It's a leap with a twist—you have to complete the twist within thirty degrees of a full rotation, and I had. That added a tenth of a point back to my score, shooting me into third place—the bronze—while pushing Ana Bărbosu of Romania from third to fourth and Sabrina Maneca-Voinea of Romania from fourth to fifth. It had all come down to less than a tenth of a point.

*   *   *

When I walked out for the medal ceremony that night, clad in my blue Team USA outfit, I felt such joy in my heart. Here were two women who had supported me and cheered me on standing right beside me: Rebeca Andrade of Brazil in first, Simone in second. I heard the crowds yelling our names, going wild in the stands for us, and I was overcome, the tears stinging my eyes. As the bronze medalist, I was the first to have my name called. *Jordan Chiles!* I thought of my grandpa and auntie Crystal. They had rooted for me every step of the way, and I knew they would have been beyond proud. This one was for them too.

Simone's name was called, and she took the second place position on the podium to roaring applause. When they called Rebeca's name and she started toward the first-place position, I turned to Simone. "Should we bow to her?"

Simone looked back at me and nodded her head yes, loving the idea.

"When?" I grinned.

"Now."

And we did. We bowed to our friend and competitor with pride. We gave her her flowers. Because we knew that this moment was history. Never before had there been an all-Black podium in Olympic women's gymnastics. And I was part of that history.

21

THIRTY-SIX MINUTES

And then, in the midst of the happiest moment of my life, I was hit with a ferocious backlash. Because Ana Bărbosu had fallen from third place after my score was corrected, Romania believed they'd been deprived (again) of a medal. And when Nadia Comăneci, one of the greatest gymnasts of her time and a Romanian icon, took it upon herself to state that her country had been deprived of its rightful bronze, many believed her. Overnight, my social media went from an outpouring of love, congratulations, and praise to hate messages and racial slurs from around the world.

SNEAKY BLACK give the medal back to the Romanian gymnast . . . she deserves it was posted under a photo of our all-Black podium on my Instagram.

This is example of fake empowerment and inclusivity. What's the problem of giving the bronze to the Romanian girl that deserved it? Oh yeah . . . she is white. Doesn't fit the agenda of inclusivity and it won't be BlAcK GiRl MaGic.

Also on my Instagram:

You are funny ape lover.

Yes, you're a nig and you were rewarded for it, we know that.

Give back the stolen medal!

Cry me a river.

GET A JOB NIGGER!

It just went on and on, as direct responses to my Instagram posts and stories and in comments on various news articles and Twitter posts. Under a CNN headline on X that read, *The celebration of an all-Black podium by Simone Biles and Jordan Chiles is highly significant for Vice President Kamala Harris,* was the comment, *Now we know why they stole the Olympic medal from Romanian gymnast Ana Bărbosu. She wasn't black enough.*

I was crushed—and angry. None of this would have happened if Ana's coach, who knew that Cécile had submitted an inquiry right after my floor routine, had waited for the inquiry results to come in before allowing Ana to take the podium, holding her flag. "Ana Bărbosu on the podium here, wow!" an NBC Sports commentator had exclaimed. That was highly unusual and premature—our coaches would not have allowed us to do that. Everyone knows you don't celebrate until after everything is final—and an inquiry for my score had been announced. "Not to throw water, guys, on the medalists' party," the other NBC commentator said, "but we've just been told that there's been an inquiry put in on Jordan Chiles's floor routine. These results, they may not stay."

The fact that the validity of my medal was being questioned after the fact—days after the medal ceremony had taken place—was surprising and outrageous to me. Once the medal ceremony has happened, that is the final result unless a drug or rules violation is discovered. That had been the case at every single Olympics in history.

And so, my family and I proceeded as if everything wasn't about to blow up in our faces. Even as we heard rumblings, through USA Gymnastics and my coaches, that Romania was upset about my win. We thought, *People are just being salty. It'll pass.* I tried to just keep going.

But I was falling apart. I had crashed from the celebratory moment of my *life* to complete desolation. A wave of self-doubt tried to push its way back to the foreground from where I'd pushed it down years before. I couldn't let it. I had to fight back. I uninstalled all of my phone's social media apps, at my mom's insistence, to avoid the venomous hate being hurled at me from what felt like everywhere. These people who had never met me were attacking my character. My family. The sheer ugliness of it was the hardest part to stomach. That people could be like this—and that they could direct that vitriol at me.

We hadn't even left France yet when the hate began, and I needed to get my mind off of it. My family and I drove to my favorite place in the midst of this hailstorm, taking a one-day trip to Disneyland Paris. But one day of fun wasn't enough to make it go away or to make me forget about it.

The day after our trip to Disney, I flew to New York to

start my media tour. This was impossibly difficult to do, acting normal when I clearly did not feel that way. We had a whole lineup of appearances to get through, including a slew of podcasts, talk shows, and magazine interviews. I stepped out of the car in Manhattan, entering the building for my interviews with *Glamour, Teen Vogue, Self,* and *GQ Sports.* My mom's phone rang as we walked into the Condé Nast building with my publicist, Noa, and my sister Jazmin as my hair and makeup artist.

"Uhhh, I gotta take this," my mom told me. "I'll catch up with you." I continued down the hallway without her, not knowing that my world was about to truly come crashing down.

I later learned that the call she was receiving was from Stefanie Korepin and Annie Heffernon at USA Gymnastics.

"Gina, we can't even explain what is happening right now" is the first thing they said to her. "We're so, so sorry, but we just got notification that the Romanian Gymnastics Federation has filed a motion against the FIG." They had filed with the Court of Arbitration for Sport (CAS), an independent organization that helps settle disputes in sports through arbitration or mediation. The International Gymnastics Federation and Donatella Sacchi herself, the head judge, had been named in the lawsuit, and I, along with USA Gymnastics and the United States Olympic & Paralympic Committee (USOPC), had been named as "interested parties." Romania was officially contesting my bronze medal win.

"We just found out about this," USA Gymnastics told my mom. "They filed this days ago, and we just got the notification because they sent it to the wrong email address.

Now, we only have forty-six minutes to put somebody in place to file the paperwork by the deadline. We really suggest that you get a lawyer."

"Wait, *what?*"

"I'm sorry, Gina, the court hearing is at eight a.m. tomorrow, Paris time." By now, it was already four p.m. New York time.

"Wait, what are you *talking* about?" My mom tried to get them to slow down. "So you mean we're going to be *asleep* when this thing happens? They're going to rule on Jordan's medal in the middle of the *night* for us?"

"Gina, we have a lawyer that we're using. We had to hire him fast, and he can represent Jordan too if you want."

"Wha—represent her? What are you talking about?!"

"Look, we know this is a lot to process. It's a lot for us too. But it's just wise to have somebody who's there to represent Jordan. It's probably just precautionary. The filing is ridiculous and we don't believe CAS could possibly rule in Romania's favor. We're sorry, we wish we had time to explain it all more fully but we need you to decide right now because we have less than an hour."

Though we were only just learning about this hearing that was set to take place the next day, CAS had refused to offer an extension when USA Gymnastics lawyers and USOPC asked. It was CAS's error that had left us in the dark until now, but they insisted the hearing had to move forward as planned because the day the hearing was set for was the day before the Olympics ended—and the panel assigned to decide the Romanians' appeal was part of CAS's Ad Hoc Division, a temporary tribunal. That panel would not be able to act once the Games were over.

My mother had been keeping as much of the dispute about my bronze medal as she could away from me because I was simply not in a state of mind to deal with it. With all the hate messages coming in, I was already beginning to retreat into myself. I was trying to fight off depression at what should have been my happiest moment. In just days, I'd gone from crumpling to my knees in joy on the arena floor to being fearful of even looking at my phone. But now a decision needed to be made, and she couldn't keep me in the dark anymore.

When she made it down the Condé Nast hallway to where I was standing with Noa and Jazmin, she looked like a duck who was calm on the surface but paddling feverishly underneath. I knew that look on her face. "Guys, can you—I need to talk to Jordan. I'm so sorry." She was stumbling over her words.

My anxiety instantly skyrocketed. I was already not having a "normal" day. I had all those media obligations ahead of me; I had to put on a brave face—and I was already struggling to do that. Now, I was about to be completely shattered. By the time my mom got to me, we had only forty-two minutes to put together the paperwork defending my Olympic win, but I didn't know that yet.

My mom grabbed me and pulled me into the nearest bathroom. My heart was pounding. What was she about to say to me? What was so important that it couldn't wait—that she'd literally snatched me out of the hallway just steps away from the *Glamour* offices?

As the words spilled from her mouth, my head spun. I felt dizzy as I struggled to keep up. *USA Gymnastics . . . my medal . . . Romanian Federation . . . lawyer . . .*

She finished in a flurry, practically out of breath. "I don't know what to do, but it's probably in your best interest to have someone there to represent you?"

Represent me . . . ?

My head felt like it was about to explode. I was already hanging on by a thread—the thinnest of threads. All I wanted to do was go back home to Texas, to my room, to my bed, and close the door on the world. But now I needed a *lawyer?*

"I—I don't know," I stammered back in response, as she looked at me expectantly. "Call Dad," was all I could manage. I knew that we would see him later that evening at the hotel, but we couldn't wait for that; we needed to talk to him now. In my family, my mom handled our day-to-day, but when there was a big decision to be made, we called Dad. So that's all I could think to do or say. That was my reflex.

By the time the phone rang and he picked up and she blurted out what was going on, we had only thirty-six minutes. Thirty-six minutes to make a decision that could change the course of my life forever. What my mother was saying, I now heard for the second time, as she recounted her call with USA Gymnastics to my dad, was that they were trying to take away my medal.

Romania wanted to strip me of the bronze.

22

NIGHTMARE TERRITORY

Thirty-six minutes is not enough time to find and hire your own lawyer, let alone one who specializes in sports law. We had to move forward with USA Gymnastics's lawyer filing our response to their suit. And then I went into my interviews and tried to act normal and laugh as we talked about makeup. The interviews were fun, but I couldn't enjoy them as I'd wanted to. Even as I gabbed with the interviewers about simple things like hair and nails, I was still wearing those medals around my neck—that was why I was there; they wanted to talk to *Jordan Chiles, the gold and bronze medalist.* But all I could think during those interviews was *I don't even know if this bronze medal is still mine.*

I sat through that day of interviews and appearances with my head absolutely spinning. I tried to remember what therapy had taught me about holding my peace and processing the unexpected, but that was hard to grasp and hang on to, hard to focus on in the middle of this hurricane that was suddenly swirling around me.

Now that we'd accepted the representation of USA Gymnastics's lawyer, and the hearing was fast approaching, just hours away, the calls started flooding in, my mom's phone ringing off the hook. Nadia Comăneci had gone to Thomas Bach, the president of the International Olympic Committee (IOC), along with the Romanian Gymnastics Federation, and the prime minister of Romania was saying that Romania would be protesting the floor bronze situation by not walking in the Olympic closing ceremonies on August 11. Heads of state were getting involved— that would be like if President Biden approached the IOC about one of its gymnasts! Nadia Comăneci declared that she was advocating on behalf of Ana's and Sabrina's mental health—but who was advocating on behalf of *my* mental health?

At the heart of Romania's challenge at this point was not Ana, the initial bronze winner, but Sabrina, who was now in fifth place. Sabrina's coach, who is also her mom, had put in an inquiry challenging Sabrina's difficulty score, and the Romanians were arguing that challenge had been improperly denied. Sabrina was not even the person who'd been dropped from the podium, Ana was, but Romania was still fighting for Sabrina—who happened to be the daughter of Nadia Comăneci's teammate and friend Camelia Voinea. Ana and Sabrina Maneca-Voinea had been tied for third place before I did my floor routine, but there was a tiebreak rule that put Ana in third: she had a higher execution score than Sabrina. If Sabrina could contest her difficulty score, then maybe she could pull ahead into third place.

But we soon learned from our lawyer that while Romania's coach had indeed challenged Sabrina's difficulty score, what the coach should have contested was the "neutral deduction" assessed because the judges said Sabrina had stepped out of bounds. A difficulty score inquiry wouldn't address that; she would have had to lodge an inquiry for a neutral deduction, and she hadn't. Within hours, the sports world and gymternet across social media reacted. *Well, if they didn't even challenge the neutral deduction, then what is Romania making all this commotion about?* What the Romanian coach had or hadn't done for their athlete had nothing to do with me. That was not my fault. And, at this point, in my mind, it was a non-challengeable call that they were now bringing up because they were sour.

The situation was snowballing out of control, seemingly hour by hour. Twelve hours before, I hadn't even had a lawyer or—as far as I was aware—the need for one, but now my mom's phone seemed permanently glued to her ear. Could Romania *really* take my medal away? "We can't tell you that it *can't* happen," the lawyer told her. "It's just *never* happened, and it *shouldn't* happen. It would be wrong if it happened, but there's nothing we can guarantee at this point." It all sounded like lawyer talk to me. What did that even *mean*?

We can't guarantee you anything.

"We can only tell you," the lawyer said, "that no one in the history of the entire Olympics, not just gymnastics, but the Olympics, has ever had a bronze medal, or a medal of any kind, stripped for something other than doping or the athlete doing something wrong. Never has anybody been stripped of a medal for doing absolutely nothing wrong." The only hope the lawyers could give us was that they felt confident because this would set a precedent. And, they felt, there's no way that the IOC and the FIG were willing to set that type of precedent. No way *that* would ever happen.

I simply could not be the one to handle the legal back and forth. I was still processing what was going on—the hate that was coming my way, a whole nation apparently against me—and I couldn't deal with the lawyers too. So my mom jumped into mom mode as I walked into interview after interview that day.

By the time we got back to the hotel that evening, I was as mentally and emotionally exhausted as I've ever been in my life. I went straight to my room, which was next door to my parents' room, and shut the door, locking myself in. On my phone were texts from friends and family—*We're seeing stuff on social media. What's going on?*—and from Cécile: *Just try to stay silent.* Simone texted, *Try to let it pass.* But my heart was aching in so many ways. I felt like I was in pieces, unable to pull myself together. I remember thinking, *Please, this is just so overwhelming.*

I'd been waffling all day between *I just want to break down and cry* and *No, Jordan, toughen up.* Now, I finally gave myself permission to release all of what I'd been feeling. I knew that I was in the middle of a storm, and I was confused by how it had developed so quickly and unexpectedly, but I had no idea if I'd already suffered the worst of the damage it would bring or if this was only the beginning. I let out all the tears I hadn't been able to throughout the day.

The hearing was only a couple of hours away, Paris time. I went to bed, putting it all in the hands of my mother. She had shielded me from so much in my life. But I wasn't sure that she could shield me from this.

* * *

At three o'clock in the morning, a cell phone rang in my parents' hotel room. I was still in a restless sleep in the room next door.

My mom sat groggily up in bed next to my dad, who was now stirring too. She reached for the phone and saw that it was the lawyer calling. His first words to her were "This is bad." He was attending the CAS hearing, now going on in Paris, remotely. Sabrina's request for the IOC to reevaluate her routine and adjust her score had been thrown out, just as we'd expected, he said. But the Romanian Federation was clearly prepared to lose on that front and had come with a plan B: they claimed that my coach, Cécile, had not challenged my score within the one-minute time limit. They said she'd put the request in one minute and twenty-four seconds after I finished my routine.

CAS now had to look into this. To verify the Romanians' assertion, the IOC referred to the arena's Omega clock records, which would show when Coach Cécile's first inquiry into my floor routine had been put into the system. But a technical assistant on the floor is responsible for entering those inquiries, leaving room for human error.

The lawyer told my mom he had to go and that he'd call her back as the hearing continued to unfold. The moment they hung up, her phone rang with back-to-back calls from Li Li Leung, the president and CEO of USA Gymnastics, and Annie Heffernon, vice president of the USA Gymnastics's women's program. It was like a hornet's nest had been kicked, and the USA Gymnastics hive was in an uproar. "Oh my gosh, what is happening?" my mom wanted to know, but they had no answers for us. They were just as confused as we were, freaking out.

"We're listening in on the trial," Li Li told my mom. "This is crazy."

She had to hang up to take another call from the lawyer. "All right, Gina, I have a question for you," he said. My mom tapped my father's arm, getting his attention, then turned back to the phone, her heart racing.

"What is it?"

"If they just award three bronze medals, would Jordan be okay with sharing?"

My mom was incredulous at this. "But Jordan is still the bronze medal winner. So they just wanna give them consolation bronze medals? Look, Jordan is asleep after a *very* rough day, and I'm not going to bother her with this. Anyway, I'm fairly certain I know what her answer would be. Jordan is a sportswoman at heart. We've taught her to be that way since she was a child. She is not going to care as long as the podium is the podium—her, Simone, and Rebeca—and she is still the bronze winner," she told them, acknowledging that I would be fine with all three of us getting medals—but there could be only one winner.

By now, my dad was up, out of bed, pacing around as my mom went from call to call, sick to her stomach at what was unfolding. When she hung up with the lawyer, my parents exchanged a worried look, glancing at each other in the darkness of the moonlit room.

"Bro, are they really trying to strip Jordan of this medal?"

My mom shook her head, worried. The tone of all of these calls didn't sound good. In fact, they seemed to be getting more and more frantic as the night went on. The phone rang again. The lawyer. My mom took a deep breath, glanced at my dad, and answered it.

The lawyer explained that the FIG and the IOC were blocking the distribution of three bronze medals. They said it would tarnish the spirit of the medal. There would be a three-hour delay in the hearing and then he could call us back with more information.

At this point, my parents decided they couldn't continue to try shielding me from the uproar. There was too much hanging in the balance. Would they wait to tell me what was happening until the bronze medal was officially taken from me—if that happened? No, they decided. They couldn't wait that long. They had to go ahead and tell me now.

*   *   *

My cell phone chimed loudly beside my head before the sun was even up. *What the* . . . I jolted awake and grabbed the phone. A text from Mom: *Can you come here?*

I immediately felt my chest tighten and clinch. *Is there an issue with our flight or something?* Maybe I was in denial, but in those first moments of being awake, it didn't occur to me that somewhere on the other side of the Atlantic, a hearing was taking place in which I was an "interested party." That was not the first thought on my mind.

I pulled myself out of bed in my pajamas and dragged the comforter from the bed, wrapping myself in it. I opened the door that joined my hotel room with my parents' and leaned against the doorjamb. I wasn't ready for it. I wasn't ready for any of it.

"What's going on?" I croaked. My voice was still filled with sleep, my eyes adjusting to the light they'd turned on in their room. I was expecting them to be like, *Okay, we missed our flight because this and the other.*

"I . . ." My mom tried to gather her words, as my dad stood looking concerned. She explained to me all that had happened while I was asleep. As she recounted the story, it hit me all over again. This was really happening. Tears streamed down my face.

When my mom finished with "I'm sorry, Jordan. This isn't looking good," what I thought was just *I want to go home.* I sputtered, "They could really take my medal from me? Like, for real?" And then I leaned my head against the wall and slid down it to the floor, just bawling. Just a lump of emotions that I couldn't even identify, and it was awful. Was it my fault? Had I done something wrong to deserve this? *What do I do now? What do I do?* But I didn't know what to do.

"Jordan. I'm so sorry, mamas," my dad tried to comfort me as I sobbed. "I know you are hurting. The world was just not ready to see that historic podium. But God has you." But I was broken, destroyed. Absurd thoughts started filling my head. *I just want to go and hide this thing. We'll tell them I don't even have it. Tell them I left the bronze in Paris.* I was thinking all sorts of things that I knew even in the moment didn't make sense. But how do you react to something like that? How do you react to being told in the middle of the night that some committee is going to strip you of your dream?

Why me, of all people? That was really my main thought. *Why me?*

"I just want to go home. Let's just—can we go home?" I kept saying over and over that I wanted to go away and disappear. But no, it was only day two of my three-day media tour. I still had two more days of events—interviews at Nike and my first meeting with my publisher—before I could go home and just close my door.

*   *   *

I put on a green-and-white Nike tennis set with a pair of tinted sunglasses and set out to face my day. We called an Uber Black SUV to whisk us off to the mall, and my mom, my sister Jazmin, my brother Ty, my dad, and I all piled in. We were all hungry and decided we'd grab food at the mall while I tried to clear my head, letting my inner sneakerhead take over. But as we were in the car, my mom's phone rang.

She was sitting right next to me, our legs touching. "It's USA Gymnastics," she said. I could feel when she tensed up.

Annie Heffernon, Li Li Leung, and Stefanie Korepin were all on the line, crying. They just kept saying, "I'm so sorry. We're so, so sorry." I was sitting so close to my mom in the car that I could hear every word.

"What?" my mom stammered. "What's going on?" I was literally not even breathing, waiting to hear what they would say.

"We don't even know how this happened! This is so wrong. This is so *wrong.*"

My body just tensed up. I was so thankful for those sunglasses since there were now tears falling from my eyes because I could see the writing on the wall before they even said it.

"They made the ruling," one of them said. "CAS ruled that Cécile was four seconds over the one-minute allotted mark, according to the Omega clock, when she went to put in the inquiry. And therefore, they are overturning the inquiry. That drops Jordan back down to fifth place. Ana will take the medal, and Sabrina will take fourth place."

Suddenly, the car went quiet. I'm surprised everyone couldn't hear the sound of my heart breaking, because it absolutely did, there in that back seat. My brain stopped even functioning with my body. Somewhere faraway, I could see my mom shaking her head, and hear her saying, "Why? *Why!*" We were still in an Uber, being driven by someone we did not know, and the only way I could react was with silent tears behind my sunglasses, as the Uber continued driving us through the streets of Manhattan.

To be honest, I'm not what I would call a vulnerable person. Expressing my feelings has always been difficult for me. Maybe everything that I've been through in my life has made me that way. But in that moment, my thoughts were just all over the place. I couldn't pick out a single thought to focus on; I just felt thrown into a hurricane and spit out the other side. When the Uber stopped and let us out, I just took off walking. I don't know if my family called out after me. I don't know if they ran to catch up with me. I just took off walking, trying to process those words. *We're so sorry. This is so wrong. The Omega clock . . . Ana will take the medal . . .*

23

NO SURRENDER

On August 10, 2024, the day before the Olympics closing ceremony in Paris, the Court of Arbitration for Sport made their decision that I should not keep my bronze medal. Following their ruling, the IOC changed the official results of the women's gymnastics floor final, and the IOC officially declared that my medal would be stripped. I had only had it for five days. Unimaginably, the best experience of my life had turned into one of the worst, and it was the purest form of devastation I'd ever felt. But I did what I always did: I pushed through. I continued on with my day, reminding myself to hold my head up high. Interviews with Nike, a meeting with my publisher for this book—I showed up for them as if nothing had happened, as if my whole world hadn't just been rocked. I tried to keep a smile on my face. I tried to conjure up that hype woman within me, even though this time, it was *me* that needed hyping, not a crowd. It was so hard not to just shut myself in a room and cry. But I told myself I could not do that. I would not do that.

The CAS ruling came down on my second day of media and meetings, and I got through them all, but then my mom canceled my remaining tour schedule in New York. I just couldn't do it for a third day. Everyone had asked about that medal, and I just couldn't talk about it anymore. I didn't even know if it was mine *to* talk about anymore. I couldn't smile and wave and answer questions when my whole world seemed to be imploding. It felt like a Mack Truck had hit me at full speed, and I needed to take a break for my own mental health. So my family and I prepared to fly home to Texas.

On that flight, my mom received a DM from Coach Cécile. *Watch this* was all she wrote, followed by a link. When my mom tapped the link, she immediately saw that it was footage from the filming that Netflix had been doing at the Paris Olympics. Film crews had been on the floor of the arena with us, capturing everything that was happening for Simone's documentary. They had been following her on and off since she got back to the gym to train for Paris, and the first two episodes of the doc came out in July, as we were gearing up for our Olympic performances. The final episodes, about her Paris Olympics showing, would drop in October.

On the last day of our competitions—that fateful August 5—the film crew had miked up Cécile so that they could capture some authentic conversations between Simone and her coach.

My mom sat on the plane watching the footage with my

dad (I wasn't sitting with them). "Sure, mike me up," Cécile says. Much of their conversation was in French, so Netflix had supplied subtitles.

In the video, you can see me leave the floor after my routine and go sit next to Simone at the kiss and cry, rubbing my stung ankles, while Cécile and Laurent confer, frantically speaking to each other in French. The announcement had been made in the arena that Sabrina's coach's inquiry into her floor final score was denied, which triggered Coach Laurent to be like, "Well, what about Simone's?" Laurent had inquired about an element of Simone's floor score *before* Sabrina's coach put hers in—like I said, those inquiries happen all the time. But there had never been an announcement about Simone's inquiry. That's when our coaches discovered that the inquiry Laurent had submitted on Simone's behalf hadn't been registered.

Laurent says in French, "They didn't do it."

"What do you mean they didn't do it?" Cécile asks him.

"She didn't do it," he responds.

Cécile turns to Simone and says, "They didn't send it," raising her arms in annoyed helplessness. They had submitted Simone's inquiry, but it was never filed. Maybe the judge didn't hear him, Laurent says, but for whatever reason the inquiry wasn't put in and Simone's routine was never reexamined.

Cécile then turns to Laurent: "What about Jordan? You want to try?"

Laurent responds in French, "Yes, go do it."

As they're having this conversation, the metadata clock is running. You can see, in the video, how long it has been since I walked off the floor and my score was posted.

You see Cécile walk away to the inquiry table. "Inquiry for Jordan," she says clearly. The metadata at the bottom of the clip is still running. *Forty-seven seconds.* It's there as clear as day: she put in my first inquiry forty-seven seconds after my score went up. The woman doesn't hear her. You hear Cécile again at the fifty-five-second mark. "Inquiry for Jordan! Inquiry for Jordan!" This time she says it twice.

The rules state that a coach must make a *verbal* inquiry within sixty seconds of the gymnast's score being announced, if they are the last gymnast in the rotation—not that the inquiry has to be *registered* within sixty seconds. That extra seventeen seconds—from the forty-seven-second mark when Coach Cécile submitted the verbal inquiry on my behalf to when that inquiry was actually registered in the Omega clock sixty-four seconds after my score was posted—was human error on the part of the official who was receiving the inquiry. During the CAS hearing, the FIG had even acknowledged that there isn't a mechanism in place to record when verbal inquiries are submitted by the coaches, only when they're registered in the system by the official in charge of them. That is obviously a huge loophole in the inquiry process (not to mention the fact that officials sometimes fail to register inquiries, as happened in Simone's case).

When Cécile comes back, Simone asks again about her own inquiry situation. They tell her that she's now past her time, that the inquiry was verbally submitted but now there's nothing they can do about it.

"For Jordan?" Simone asks, looking for clarification.

"No, for you," Laurent says.

As this conversation is going on between Laurent and

Simone, my eyes glance up at the leaderboard. My new score goes up, and I scream as I leap into Cécile's arms. You can hear her say, "Oh, Jordan! Oh, Jordan!" thrilled for me. Her inquiry had worked! It was as if we had won the world. And, in that moment, it truly felt like we had.

My parents got super excited after watching this filmed evidence. They showed me after we landed, and I couldn't believe my eyes. Cécile had told them she'd immediately sent the link to USAG and our lawyers as well. I just knew that we were going to get justice this time—no doubt about it!

After reviewing the footage, our lawyers sent a notice to CAS appealing the ruling that had stripped me of the bronze. Now there was video evidence, provided by the production company Religion of Sports themselves, showing that I should have never been stripped of the bronze medal in the first place. We had not had this information when the hearing took place. We had it now.

CAS was unmoved. They came back the next day with a crushing response: *USA Gymnastics was notified by the Court of Arbitration for Sport [CAS] on Monday that their rules do not allow for an arbitral award to be reconsidered even when conclusive new evidence is presented.* CAS had seen the video and knew that what we said was true, but the Olympics were over, so the CAS Ad Hoc Division was no longer in existence. They'd rushed to have the hearing before the Olympics ended, allowing us only hours to prepare a case, then denied my appeal once conclusive evidence was presented in support of me. We ultimately learned that the rushed timeline hadn't been necessary. The Ad Hoc Division's panels could only rule while the Olympics were in session, but our appeal could have been heard according to the normal CAS procedures and timeline. Rushing it ensured it was the temporary panel that would have final say—and the head of that three-person panel, Dr. Hamid Gharavi, had represented Romania in multiple arbitration cases, which called into question whether he was really impartial.

USAG lawyers advised that we file an appeal with the Swiss tribunal, the highest court you can go to for sports disputes. Now I had pro bono lawyers coming out of the woodwork from all over, champing at the bit to take on my case. They all thought that they could be the ones to steer us to success. We knew that we needed to get a separate lawyer from USA Gymnastics, who were planning to file their own suit with the Swiss tribunal. We needed to be sure we had someone solely interested in representing my best interests. If conflicts of interest arose between me and the governing body for the sport of gymnastics in the US, I didn't want to be caught in that cross fire.

Nike put us in touch with Gibson Dunn, one of the best legal teams in the world. We felt comfortable with them. With our legal team in place, along with a second team familiar with Swiss law, I was ready to go to war. My family and I felt bolstered by the fact that the IOC and FIG were already under tremendous media pressure. USA Today had written a series of scathing articles in my defense: *Jordan Chiles could also get a bronze if IOC wanted to do it. In Jordan Chiles's case, IOC has precedent to hand out two bronze medals. In stripping Jordan Chiles of her bronze medal, the IOC is not following the precedent it set for itself.* Then, two days later, the Washington Post published their own blistering article: *The push to strip Jordan Chiles of her Olympic medal smells awfully foul. The court that ruled against Jordan Chiles is a hive of cronies and insiders, established and steered by the IOC and various sports federations as cover.*

But I was in a fragile place, and I knew I couldn't also bear the onslaught of whatever was coming my way online. I had deleted my social media apps, but my parents and siblings were still seeing an avalanche of racially driven hatred toward me. I decided to make my social media sabbatical official.

On August 15, 2024, I posted four broken heart emojis to my Instagram story and announced that I would be stepping back from my online presence for a while as I took time to heal. *I have no words,* I wrote. *This decision feels unjust and comes as a significant blow, not just to me, but to everyone who has championed my journey. To add to the heartbreak, the unprompted racially driven attacks on social media are wrong and extremely hurtful. I've poured my heart and soul into this sport and I am so proud to represent my culture and my country.*

Luckily I had plenty to keep me busy as my legal team tried to explore every option to restore my medal. I had been asked to walk in New York Fashion Week in September, and I had an entire lineup of media appearances scheduled in the city. I also still had the bronze medal.

All of the chatter online about the medal being "taken" from me and "given" to Ana right after the Olympics was, in fact, only partly true. Because we were contesting it, the CAS decision was still technically up in the air, so the physical medal was still in my possession, and it was never requested from me—so I never gave it back. But I knew that a decision of some kind would eventually be made: either I would be allowed to keep the bronze medal with the overturning of the CAS decision, or the unthinkable would happen, and it would really be physically stripped from me. At this point, my fight was more about the principle than the medal itself. I wanted my score restored because I did *earn* it. And I wanted to make sure no other athlete would ever be stripped of a medal they had won fair and square. It was about speaking up and standing firm.

Our lawyers decided to go ahead with taking the case all the way to the Swiss tribunal. The tribunal allows procedural arguments rather than direct contesting of the facts of a case, and we had our procedural arguments ready. For example, we hadn't had the proper time to prepare a case because the notifications of the hearing were sent to the wrong email address. If we could get the court to acknowledge those deficiencies in procedure, they could reopen the CAS case and we could enter Netflix's video evidence. Then they would have no choice but to restore the podium and my bronze medalist status.

Statistically, the Swiss tribunal has a success rate of less than 8 percent—that's how hard it is to win. I was willing to take my chances. Whether or not we won, having this case heard—both in the Swiss tribunal and in the court of public opinion—had the potential to change how the IOC and the FIG conducted business for future athletes. I could make that stand. I could push for that change.

EPILOGUE

On Wednesday, September 11, I sat down with Moira Forbes at the 2024 Forbes Power Women's Summit at Lincoln Center in New York City. It was my first time speaking out since I'd been stripped of the bronze medal. Interview requests had been pouring in from all of the big names in media, but I wasn't ready to fully dive into what had happened. We were still fighting—I didn't know if I would emerge at the end of that tunnel with recognition as an individual bronze medalist for my country. But even though nothing had been settled, I finally decided to sit down with Moira. I was thrumming with nerves the entire time backstage beforehand. I kept mouthing to my mom, who stood beside me, *I'm so nervous. I'm so nervous.*

"You're going to be fine," she reassured me. "Just go out there and speak from your heart."

So I did. I told Moira, "At this rate, it's not really about the medal. It's about my peace and my justice." The audience applauded, and I knew within myself that it was true, and I was glad I'd said it.

"You said things were taken from you," Moira said. "What was taken from you?" I had to pause to collect myself then. Because so much had been taken from me, from the moment Coach X began controlling my life to all the microaggressions I'd experienced along the way. There was no way I could have expressed just how much in that one answer.

I took a deep breath. "The biggest thing that was taken from me was the recognition of who I was," I told her, fighting back tears. "Not just my sport but the person I am. To me, everything that has gone on is not about the medal. It's about my skin color."

Would Romania have challenged my win, would the CAS have ruled differently, if I were a white athlete? There's no way to know, and that was part of my point. When a sport is as racist as gymnastics has long been, you can't rule out skin color as a possible factor in any aspect of competition—and that poisons everything. What has been taken from me—from all of us, really—is our trust that fairness will prevail. But the hurt I was feeling was no longer about the medal. It was about all of the racial hate and backlash I'd received over the years, and the brutal backlash surrounding the bronze medal in particular. That's what I was trying to get across in my Power Women's Summit interview. After that interview, the backlash only got worse. *Jordan Chiles pulls the race card. You're disgusting. I supported you and now I never will again because you used race as your reason. You're really such a loser making it about race. Aren't Simone and Rebeca Black too—what are you talking about?*

I saw these comments online even though I'd deleted all my apps. These people had no idea of the hate I'd been facing, or that my race *had* been at the center of so much of the controversy that surrounded me in the sport.

Later that same day I was set to present the VMA Award for Best Collaboration, alongside the legendary Flavor Flav. After a hectic afternoon of switching venues, then hair and wardrobe changes, I sat backstage going over my lines. When I heard the cheers erupting from the crowd as my name was called to come out onstage, it really threw me. All the love the public was showing me. Chanting my name in support. To tell you the truth, for a second I forgot the lines I had memorized!

I stepped out to a roar of applause, the exact opposite of the comments that were multiplying online in that very moment. I wanted to take it all in.

"I know they tried to take your medal away from you," Flavor Flav told me, in that distinctive voice of his. "I got you something that they can't take away from you." Then he stepped behind me to clasp a big crystal-encrusted bronze stopwatch necklace, almost exactly like the one he's famous for wearing, around my neck. This was nowhere in our script, and now I was completely thrown off, but in all the best ways. The way the crowd applauded, the way they screamed our names and were so happy that he'd done this for me. I felt so much love and support from him and the audience, something I'd spoken about being deprived of just hours before with Moira Forbes. "Wow, I don't even know what to say here!" I replied, still in this most wonderful kind of shock. "Thank you so much!"

That moment was so overwhelming for me. I'd gone from being an athlete who'd had to fight for every shred of respect I was given in my sport, to now being in everyone's living room across the country. Suddenly, people who didn't even follow gymnastics or the Olympics knew who I was. Just being offered the chance to give out an award at the VMAs was absolutely huge for me, and when I found out that I was going to be doing it with Flav—the original hype man!—I was so excited. So, *so* excited.

For me, it became more about being in that moment than performing that segment perfectly. Flavor Flav was giving *me* a clock like his—a different kind of bronze medal! That was something that I really needed and a moment I will truly always cherish. I'll *always* have that bronze clock, and I'll always remember that night.

*   *   *

On September 16, we started our Gold Over America Tour at Frontwave Arena in Oceanside, California. This was the second time I'd participated in this gymnastics-themed tour, which celebrates the sport and Team USA's accomplishments at the Olympics. We were set to visit thirty arenas across America this time around. I arrived in Oceanside on September 13 and had only seventy-two hours to learn all of the choreography—but I did, and we had the most amazing opening show.

As I stepped out onto the stage with my fellow Olympic gymnasts that first night, I felt a little part of my heart heal. This wasn't about the bronze medal, or the still-uncertain outcome of our Swiss tribunal appeal; this was me being able to dance and perform and have fun side by side with Simone and other amazing gymnasts who knew exactly what it was like to go through some of what I'd been through. It was our time to celebrate what we had accomplished through choreography that was all personality and fun—rather than strict scoring standards and the eyes of judges. We were being cheered on by families and kids who looked up to us, and it felt amazing to remember I've become a role model for other girls. I was exhausted from all of the traveling and performing, but I found myself smiling more and more every day. No more closing myself in my room and isolating. I was right where I belonged.

What I want *all* gymnasts to recognize is that gymnastics is only worth doing if our hearts are truly in it—if we love it. And I want all young gymnasts—especially the ones who look like me—to know that you can excel in the sport without hating your body or your hair. Without tearing yourself down and dulling that inner voice that says *you are amazing just the way you are.*

To be on the international stage in front of millions while hating who you are is an experience I wouldn't wish on anyone. To feel hyper-seen but never heard. To be expected to execute awe-inspiring flips through the air with grace and a smile, in the face of a system designed to extract medals without caring for the person winning them. But I'm done biting my tongue. I'm done going along with that status quo. I envision a world where the cost of admission for being an athlete isn't our sanity and sense of self worth.

Last year, I saw a video online of a young Black gymnast in Ireland being passed over during a medal ceremony. It was chillingly familiar: so similar to what I'd gone through at my own childhood medal ceremony when the plaque I'd earned was snatched from me. Every other girl at this Irish gym was white, and every one of them was given a medal, but the Black girl was intentionally skipped by the white official handing out the honors. What really stuck with me was how the girl remained so composed. She smiled, even as the hurt showed in her eyes. It reminded me of how I'd tried to make myself small every time racist parents, coaches, or institution heads berated me. Every time I was made to feel less than, or ugly, or fat. Watching that little girl in that video was like staring into a mirror.

That girl and her parents received a written letter of apology—the kind I know so well. I know those placating words, and that they can never erase the pain. The video reaffirmed for me that I needed to make my voice heard. I needed to remind Black and brown girls everywhere that they shouldn't have to negotiate for their happiness. This book is a love letter to all the world's Black and brown girls, who should not have to endure what I did.

After so many years of being silenced and forced into dark corners, I now feel so much brighter. I once thought I needed to choose between my own happiness and my sport. I now know that is not the case. You can have your cake and eat it too. You can be happy and be great at the same time. And you can show your joy: smiling and laughing does not mean you lack focus, as I was taught.

My version of gymnastics challenges the old norm. I don't look like the gymnastics stars of decades past, and I stand proud in that knowledge—with every strong, capable fiber of my five-foot-tall being. I reject the idea that I have to conform to the rigidity of my sport or of society's expectations.

When *anyone* asks you to tone it down, to make yourself small so those around you will feel more comfortable, don't listen. Instead, make your gifts so loud that they can't ignore you.

I will not be ignored. Ever again. And these words on the page are the echo of my voice.

ACKNOWLEDGMENTS

As I look back on this journey, I know that I would not be here today without the people who have poured their love, support, and strength into me, building me up to be not just a powerful athlete but a better person.

To *God*, the real MVP.

To *Mom & Dad*, you are the core of everything I am. Mom, your belief in me has been my compass. You've seen the best in me—even when I couldn't see it myself—and your strength has been my foundation. So many times, you asked me who I was, and you have challenged me to be my authentic self always. You taught me that my dreams are mine and no one but me can decide what to do with them. Dad, thank you for the endless sacrifices, for every pep talk, and for teaching me that sometimes the hard way is the best way. You are the reason I wrote a memoir because you always told me, when good *or* bad happened in my life, that it would all be chapters in my book. Your love of God and desire for Him to work through me helped me navigate this crazy life of mine. You both raised me to dream big, work hard, love people, and stay humble.

To *my grandparents, aunts, uncles, cousins,* and everyone who has shown up, celebrated, and supported me along the way—thank you for being my steady circle of love. Your presence and prayers, whether in person or from afar, have been a constant source of strength. Every hug, every message, every proud cheer from the stands or from home means so much to me. I am grateful beyond words for a family that shows up in every way, reminding me that this journey is never mine alone. I carry each of you with me every time I step onto the competition floor, feeling your love and encouragement. Uncle Joe, you are my biggest supporter, and you believed in me so much you called me an Olympian at the age of seven. You showed up for me in ways that I'll always hold close. Thank you for being there until I became *Jordan Lucella Elizabeth Olympic Gold Medalist Chiles.*

To *Jazmin & Jade,* my big sisters, you are my go-to people for everything! Thank you for not only making sure I look my best, but for helping me be my best too. You both know me like no one else and you have no problem keeping me grounded with your big sis lectures, but you have no idea how much I listen and need it. Your steady presence means the world to me, and I am thankful for your sacrifices so that I can pursue my dreams. Having you both working alongside me is priceless even though I know it can be difficult sometimes. Everything you do helps me shine.

To *Taj & Ty,* you both bring lightness and humor to my

life, reminding me to stay positive, no matter what. Thank you for always believing in me and for cheering me on with every ounce of your hearts. If you could give me the world, I know you would. I can feel how proud you are of me, and I still always want to make you proud. There are so many times I need to hear it from my big brothers, and you don't hold back, and I appreciate that. I know you have my back and stand ten toes down for your baby sis.

To *Laurent* Landi *and* Cécile Canqueteau-Landi, who have been like second parents to me through this journey. I never thought I could trust coaches again, but you both showed me I was more than just a gymnast. Thank you for bringing out the confidence I lacked and for allowing me to be me even if it didn't line up with the norm. Thank you for challenging me, for expecting my best, and for teaching me to expect the same from myself. You've pushed me to see what I'm capable of. Your compassion and wisdom have seen me through some of my hardest days, and I'm grateful for your helping me to be stronger, both on and off the mat. Thank you for helping me love gymnastics again. You are the *dopest* people I know.

And to *Simone*, my best friend and my big sister in this crazy world of gymnastics. You set this all in motion when you offered me a way to my dream when I didn't know I wanted it anymore. You've taught me so much, from the true meaning of courage to the simple freedom of speaking up. You've shown me how to embrace who I am, and you've been a rock when I needed someone to lean on. We both cried some real tears on this journey! Thank you for your friendship, your support, and for setting an example that I'm forever proud to follow. Biles and Chiles forever.

To *my team*, I have no idea how to thank you for believing in me through two Olympic cycles and for always focusing on what I love. You have successfully pushed others to see me with the same eyes you see me with. You believe I can move mountains, and you make me feel unstoppable. Meanwhile, you are the ones moving mountains on my behalf. I prayed for people to help guide me like you all have done and I'm forever proud to work with you. Amy Neben and Lex Maitland and the Select Team, Noa Rocco and Laura Potesta and the R&CPMK team—you all are family in my eyes.

To *Dimitri*, I am grateful for you, your belief in me, and for being the peace in the storm that kept me going when my dream felt the furthest away.

To Lisa Sharkey and the team at HarperCollins—Maddie Pillari, Lexie von Zedlitz, Robin Bilardello, Bonni Leon-Berman, Becca Putnam, Kate d'Esmond, Beth Silfin—and to Jacklyn Saferstein-Hansen and Alan Nevins at Renaissance Literary & Talent, thank you for believing in my story and for wanting to share it with the world. To Felice Laverne and Kim Hubbard, what a whirlwind these last few months have been. You all helped me tell my story in a way that seemed impossible. Thank you for pulling out what lived inside of me all of these years.

To Maurice Suh, Al Suarez, Zach Freund and the Gibson, Dunn & Crutcher team, and Gabrielle Nater-Bass and the Homburger team—thank you for being an extension of my voice in my fight for justice in a crazy storm.

To everyone who has been there for me—my friends, my teammates, sponsors, Lori Roth, Ann Miller and my entire Nike family, my fans, and those who have supported me behind the scenes, you are part of my story, my journey. This is not just my achievement; it's ours. I thank you all, with every bit of my heart.

ABOUT THE AUTHOR

Jordan Chiles is an American gymnast, a member of the US National Gymnastics Team, and a member of the UCLA gymnastics team. The youngest of five children, Chiles was named after Michael Jordan and began gymnastics at age six and a half, when her parents signed her up for classes at a gym near their Vancouver, Washington, home. She rose through the ranks quickly, developing the powerful vault and dynamic floor routine for which she is now known. She was a member of the silver medal-winning team at the 2020 Tokyo Olympics and a member of the team that won gold at the 2022 World Championships; later that year she shifted to the collegiate level, becoming an NCAA athlete at UCLA and a two-time NCAA National Champion before putting her studies on hold to focus on the 2024 Paris Olympics. There, she made "I'm that girl" her motto—a way to remind herself that, whatever the challenge, she always shows up and gives it her all.

FIRST EDITION

Designed by Leah Carlson-Stanisic

Title page:
1. Credit line: © Lionel Bonaventure/Getty Images
2. Credit line: © Paul Ellis/Getty Images
3. Credit line: John Cheng
4. Credit line: © Lionel Bonaventure/Getty Images
5. Credit line: © Carmen Mandato/Getty Images

Image following title page: Asatur Yesayants/Shutterstock, inc.

All photographs in the insert are courtesy of the author unless otherwise noted.

Library of Congress Cataloging-in-Publication Data has been applied for.

ISBN 978-0-06-344340-2

24 25 26 27 28 LBC 5 4 3 2 1